Praise

"**I received personalized financial advice that helped me select investment options aligned with my risk tolerance**. The financial advisor's expertise was invaluable in navigating the complexities of different investment instruments. Their guidance allowed me to make informed decisions and build a suitable investment portfolio."

~ Mr. Tamilselvan (Project Manager with over 15 years of IT industry experience)

"**His financial advisor team excels at simplifying the complex world of investing.** They possess a deep understanding of various investment vehicles and strategies, enabling them to tailor portfolios to individual risk profiles. By conducting a thorough assessment of clients' financial goals, risk tolerance, and time horizon, the team effectively navigates the investment landscape, identifying optimal opportunities that align with their clients' unique circumstances. This personalized approach fosters trust and confidence, allowing clients to relax knowing their financial future is in capable hands."

~ Mr. Kaarthick (Tech Architect with over 13 years of experience)

"**Parthiban is an exceptional financial advisor who offers invaluable insights and guidance.** His deep understanding of financial matters is evident in the practical and effective suggestions he provides. He has a remarkable ability to break down complex financial concepts into easily understandable terms, making him an excellent educator.

Parthiban's advice has proven to be instrumental in helping individuals make informed decisions about their finances. His recommendations are tailored to specific needs and goals, demonstrating his personalized approach to financial planning. Moreover, he fosters a learning environment, empowering clients to take control of their financial future."

~ Mr. Ram Kumar (Senior RM with 10 years of banking experience)

Money Gravity

A Journey through Planning, Mindset, Safety Nets, and Wise Investments.

Author

Parthiban Viswanathan

(Financial Freedom Coach)

Table of Contents

Praise 1

Foreword 7

Preface 9

Introduction 11

Chapter 1: Understanding Financial Freedom 13

Chapter 2: Millionaire Mindset 22

Chapter 3: Understanding Financial Markets.. 39

Chapter 4: Emergency Funds 59

Chapter 5: Mastering Debt Management and Credit Health.. 67

Chapter 6: Different Income Types 89

Chapter 7 – Insurance................................. 98

Chapter 8 - Investment 118

Chapter 9 - Retirement Planning................... 168

Chapter 10 - Estate Planning......................... 174

Chapter 11 - Stock Market Trading 180

Chapter 12 - AI Tools 207

Chapter 13 - Multiple Sources of Income 217

Chapter 14 - Real estate 221

Chapter 15 - Tax Planning 231

Chapter 16 - Cyber Crimes and Scams.......... 241

Charity: A Cornerstone of Humanity 247

About Author.. 248

Foreword

In today's rapidly evolving world, achieving financial freedom has become an aspiration that drives individuals toward greater security, fulfillment, and empowerment. Yet, navigating the intricacies of financial management can often seem overwhelming, especially amid economic uncertainties and technological transformations.

This comprehensive guide serves as a powerful resource, meticulously designed to equip you with essential insights and practical tools necessary for your journey toward financial independence. Each chapter unfolds critical concepts ranging from developing a millionaire mindset to understanding complex financial markets, providing you with clarity and actionable strategies.

Whether it's building an emergency fund to shield yourself against unforeseen financial challenges or mastering debt management to reclaim your financial health, every aspect covered in this book aims to strengthen your financial foundation. Topics such as diverse income streams, strategic investments across stocks, mutual funds, gold, and real estate, as well as robust retirement and estate planning, ensure you're well-prepared at every stage of your financial life cycle.

I commend you for taking this vital step toward financial empowerment. May this book inspire you, guide you, and ultimately empower you to realize your financial goals and dreams with confidence and clarity.

Wishing you abundant success on your path to financial freedom.

By
Mr. Rajmohan V,
Financial expert with 15 years of industry experience.

Preface

From Novice to Financial Coach: A Journey of Empowerment

Ten years ago, I began my financial journey with little knowledge, investing my savings haphazardly and dabbling in high-risk trades. Lacking strategy and unaware of the insurance I needed, I took advice from friends without understanding the risks. The COVID pandemic highlighted the dire need for solid financial planning and insurance, as many faced loss and economic hardship. My rural roots and outsider status in finance initially held me back, but mentorship changed the game. I pursued formal education, earning certifications in retirement planning, mutual fund, insurance; learning about long-term investments and the protective power of insurance.

I discovered that passive income is the key to financial freedom. With dedication, I mastered the intricacies of investments and insurance, becoming self-reliant in managing my finances.

Now, as a Financial Freedom Coach, I've left behind a lucrative corporate job for a fulfilling mission: to lead professionals to financial independence with straightforward, efficient strategies.

The pandemic made me rethink my finances. What about you? Did it make you prioritize saving more, exploring new income streams, or something else entirely?

Introduction

Welcome to "Money Gravity: A Journey through Planning, Mindset, Safety Nets, and Wise Investments." This book helps you gain the necessary knowledge and tools to control your financial future.

Financial freedom is not just a buzzword. It is a life-changing concept that can transform your life from a constant struggle to make ends meet to a peaceful journey with a secure future. It is about having the freedom to make choices, like the choice to retire early or the choice to pursue a passion without worrying about your time and income.

But how do you become financially free? This book is loaded with practical guidance and strategies to help you start your journey towards financial independence. It is not just about managing your money; it is also about growing it.

This book will provide you with a roadmap to financial freedom. From understanding the concept of financial freedom to learning how to create a budget, save money, invest wisely, and make informed financial decisions, this guide covers it all.

I want to thank my mentors, family members, clients and everybody who has shown faith in me. Special thanks to my brother Mr. Rajmohan for reviewing the book and providing valuable insights.

Chapter 1: Understanding Financial Freedom

Financial freedom is the state of being free from the worries of living paycheck to paycheck, the worries about paying bills, or the fear of unexpected financial emergencies. It's having enough savings, investments, and cash on hand to afford the lifestyle you want for yourself and your family.

To achieve financial freedom, you need to understand it first. Understand what it means to you. Is it about being debt-free? Is it about being able to retire early? Or maybe, it's about not depending on a 9-5 job for your survival.

Benefits of Achieving Financial Freedom

1. **Improved Quality of Life:** Financial freedom allows you to pursue your passions, travel, and spend quality time with family and friends. You can afford to take time off work and focus on personal growth, leading to a more fulfilling and satisfying life.
2. **Increased Peace of Mind:** Knowing that you have enough money to cover expenses and

emergencies brings peace of mind. It positively impacts your mental and emotional well-being, reducing stress and anxiety.

3. **Reduced Stress:** Financial stress is a significant source of strain for many people. Achieving financial freedom means less worry about bills, debts, and day-to-day expenses.

4. **Control Over Your Money:** Financial freedom gives you more control over your finances. You can make better financial decisions and explore investment opportunities for additional income and long-term security.

In summary, financial freedom isn't just about wealth; it's about having the freedom to live life on your terms, unencumbered by financial limitations.

Why Financial Planning?

In today's fast-paced world, where financial responsibilities and opportunities abound, having a well-defined financial plan is crucial for achieving your life goals and securing a stable future. Let's explore why financial planning matters:

1. Smoother Transition into Different Life Stages: As we move from one life stage to another, our priorities and responsibilities change. Financial planning helps us understand our goals better and how they impact other aspects of our lives and finances. Whether it's buying a home, starting a family, or planning for retirement, a well-thought-out financial plan ensures a smoother transition across life stages.

2. Emergency Preparedness: Creating an emergency fund is a critical aspect of financial planning. Unexpected events like medical emergencies, job loss, or natural disasters can disrupt our lives. Having a financial safety net allows us to handle such situations without compromising our financial stability.

3. Tax Efficiency: Proper financial planning helps optimize tax strategies. By understanding tax laws, deductions, and credits, individuals can minimize their tax liability and keep more of their hard-earned money. Tax planning is an integral part of financial well-being.

4. Peace of Mind: Knowing that you have a plan in place provides peace of mind. Financial planning allows you to set realistic goals, track progress, and adjust as needed. It reduces anxiety about the unknown and empowers you to make informed decisions.

5. Risk Management: Financial planning involves assessing risks and protecting against them. Whether through insurance policies or investment diversification, managing risk ensures stability and resilience in the face of uncertainties.

In summary, financial planning isn't just about numbers; it's about aligning your financial choices with your life aspirations and securing a brighter future.

Case Study - MS Dhoni's Winning Formula for Financial Planning: A Wolf Pack Approach

"In an interview, Dhoni shared his secret to consistent success across various cricket formats: the wolf-pack strategy. Just as wolves organize themselves for optimal travel, we too can apply this principle to our financial lives. Start by securing your 'bulk and old wolves'—emergency funds, insurance coverage, and essential investments. Then, let the 'young and energetic wolves'—growth-oriented investments—follow. Finally, ensure that the 'middle weak ones'—less critical expenses—are taken care of. By planning ahead, we can navigate life's challenges without stress."

Remember, just like Dhoni trusts his bowlers, trust your financial plan to guide you toward victory!

From Legacy to Lawsuit: Why Succession Planning Matters?

In the world of high-stakes business, the story of the Ambani brothers stands as a stark reminder of the importance of watertight financial planning, especially for family-run enterprises. Dhirubhai Ambani, the visionary founder of Reliance Industries, built an empire that stretched across

Indian industry. Yet, his legacy was marred by a bitter public dispute between his sons, Mukesh, and Anil, following his death in 2002.

The core of the conflict stemmed from the absence of a clear succession plan. Dhirubhai reportedly left no legal will, assuming his sons would work together seamlessly. This assumption proved disastrous.

Without a documented plan outlining leadership roles and asset distribution, the brothers clashed over control of the Reliance empire. The disagreement spilled into the public eye, raising concerns about transparency and ultimately leading to a complex division of the company in 2005.

This real-life drama offers valuable lessons for any family business owner. Let's explore the crucial aspects of financial planning that the Ambani case underscores:

- **The Necessity of a Will:** A will is the cornerstone of a solid estate plan. It clearly outlines your wishes for asset distribution, minimizing ambiguity and potential conflict among heirs.

- **Open Communication:** Family business owners should have open and honest conversations with their children or designated successors. Discuss your vision for the future of the company, leadership roles, and expectations.
- **Formalized Agreements:** Don't rely on assumptions or unspoken agreements. Formalize succession plans and ownership structures through legal documents like shareholder agreements or buy-sell provisions. These documents can help mediate disputes and ensure a smoother transition.

By taking these steps, you can create a roadmap for the future of your family business, safeguarding your legacy and preventing the kind of turmoil that befell the Reliance empire. Remember, even the most successful businesses can crumble under the weight of internal conflict.

The Ambani story serves as a powerful cautionary tale, urging family business owners to prioritize meticulous financial planning. It's a testament to the fact that clear communication, legal documentation, and a well-defined succession plan

are not just recommendations, but essential ingredients for a thriving and harmonious family business.

FOOD FOR THOUGHT

"Financial freedom isn't just about money; it's about the freedom to choose your life."

Chapter 2: Millionaire Mindset

The **Millionaire Mindset** is a collection of beliefs, practices, and habits that successful entrepreneurs and individuals who have achieved financial freedom share. It is a mindset that propels individuals from ordinary to extraordinary and is characterized by several key traits

The **millionaire mindset** isn't just about money; it's a powerful way of thinking that can help you achieve your goals. Here are **10 habits** associated with this mindset:

1. **Focus on Your Goals**: Keep your objectives in mind and write them down. Regularly remind yourself of what you're working toward, even on challenging days.
2. **Embrace Lifelong Learning**: Be open to learning and adapting. Recognize that there's always something new to discover and improve upon. Celebrate the skills you acquire along the way.
3. **Step Out of Your Comfort Zone**: Networking and self-presentation are crucial. Boldly express your passion and connect with like-

minded individuals. Remember, courage and confidence leave a lasting impression.

4. **Think Abundantly**: Shift your perspective from scarcity to abundance. Believe that success is attainable and that you have the power to shape your financial destiny.

5. **Positive Money Mindset**: Nurture a growth mindset. Reframe limiting beliefs about money and success. By doing so, you open yourself up to opportunities for financial growth.

6. **Adapt to Change**: Wealthy individuals are flexible and willing to switch strategies. Embrace change and recognize that being a beginner is part of the journey.

7. **Practice Discipline**: Long-term thinking pays off. Avoid impulsive decisions and stay committed to your goals.

8. **Overcome Fear**: Fear can hold you back. Acknowledge it, but don't let it paralyze you. Take calculated risks and move forward.

9. **Give Back**: Generosity is a hallmark of the millionaire mindset. Whether through charity or mentorship, contribute positively to others' lives.

10. **Visualize Success**: Imagine yourself achieving your goals. Visualization can

reinforce your determination and pave the way for actual success.

Remember, the millionaire mindset isn't just about wealth—it's about adopting a mindset that propels you toward your dreams.

The Strangest Secret in the World

Influential audio recording by Earl Nightingale

As you embark on your journey to achieve early financial freedom, it's crucial to equip yourself with the right mindset and tools. One powerful resource that can significantly enhance your path is Earl Nightingale's **"The Strangest Secret in the World."** This pioneering audio recording has transformed the lives of millions by revealing a simple yet profound truth: "We become what we think about."

In "The Strangest Secret," Nightingale distills decades of wisdom into actionable insights that can help you set and achieve your financial goals. By listening to this recording, you will learn how to harness the power of your thoughts, set clear and compelling goals, and maintain a positive attitude even in the face of challenges.

Consider the impact that such timeless wisdom could have on your journey. Many people have found that incorporating Nightingale's principles into their daily routine has led to remarkable changes in their financial and personal lives. Don't just take my word for it—explore the testimonials of those who have listened and experienced incredible transformations.

Ready to discover these secrets for yourself? You can easily access "The Strangest Secret in the World" on platforms like YouTube, often for free. Take the first step towards unlocking your potential and achieving the financial freedom you desire. Listen today, and let the journey begin.

Financial Goal Setting

Financial goal setting is a crucial component of achieving financial freedom and long-term financial stability. It involves defining specific, measurable, achievable, relevant, and time-bound (SMART) objectives that guide your financial decisions and actions. Here's a detailed overview of how to effectively set financial goals.

Why Financial Goal Setting is Important?

1. **Clarity and Direction**:
Setting financial goals provides a clear roadmap for your financial journey. It helps you understand where you are headed and what you need to do to get there.

2. **Motivation**:
Well-defined goals can be highly motivating. They give you something to strive for and a sense of purpose.

3. **Measurement of Progress**:
Goals allow you to track your progress and make adjustments as needed. You can celebrate milestones and stay motivated.

4. **Better Decision Making**:
Having specific financial goals helps you make informed decisions that align with your long-term objectives.

5. **Financial Security**:
Achieving financial goals can lead to greater financial security and peace of mind, knowing you are on track to meet your needs and aspirations.

Steps for Effective Financial Goal Setting

1. **Assess Your Current Financial Situation**: Evaluate your income, expenses, debts, assets, and savings. Understanding your current financial position is essential for setting realistic goals.

2. **Define Your Goals**:

i). Short-term Goals (1 year or less):
- Examples: Building an emergency fund, paying off a credit card, saving for a vacation.

ii). Medium-term Goals (1-5 years):
- Examples: Buying a car, saving for a down payment on a house, paying off student loans.

iii). Long-term Goals (5+ years):
- Examples: Retirement savings, funding children's education, buying a second home.

3. **Make Your Goals SMART**:
- **Specific**: Clearly define what you want to achieve.
- **Measurable**: Establish criteria for measuring progress.
- **Achievable**: Ensure your goals are realistic and attainable.
- **Relevant**: Align your goals with your values and long-term objectives.

- **Time-bound**: Set a deadline for achieving your goals.

4. **Prioritize Your Goals**:
- Rank your goals based on importance and urgency. This helps you focus your resources on the most critical objectives.

5. **Create an Action Plan**:
- Outline the steps needed to achieve each goal. This may include creating a budget, increasing income, reducing expenses, or making specific investments.

6. **Monitor and Adjust**:
- Regularly review your progress and make adjustments as needed. Life circumstances can change, and your goals may need to be adapted.

We can use apps like Mint, YNAB (You Need A Budget), or Personal Capital that assist in tracking income, expenses, and assets.

Tips for Staying on Track

1. **Automate Savings and Investments**:
- Set up automatic transfers to your savings and investment accounts to ensure consistent progress.
2. **Track Spending**:
- Use budgeting apps or tools to monitor your expenses and identify areas where you can save more.
3. **Seek Professional Advice**:
- Consider working with a financial advisor to create a personalized plan and get expert guidance.
4. **Stay Informed**:
- Continuously educate yourself about personal finance, investments, and market trends.
5. **Stay Flexible**:
- Be prepared to adjust your goals and plans as needed to accommodate changes in your life and financial situation.

By setting clear and actionable financial goals, you can take control of your financial future, make informed decisions, and steadily work towards achieving financial freedom and security.

Case Study - The Pursuit of Excellence: From the Track to Financial Security

Unwavering Athlete:
- **P.T. Usha**'s lightning-fast sprints captivated audiences, pushing the boundaries of human performance.
- Usha's mastery of hurdles and her triumphant finish line crossing embodied determination and excellence.

Dedicated Training:
- Usha's renowned rigorous training and unwavering focus honed her skills and endurance.
- Her resilience and persistence shone through setbacks, refusing to be deterred from her goals.

Legendary Achievements:
- Usha's dominance at the Asian Games and multiple world records solidified her as a sporting icon.
- Despite narrowly missing an Olympic medal, Usha's legacy extended beyond her athletic accomplishments.

Empowering Security:
- Insurance coverage offers families the peace of mind to pursue their dreams without financial worries.

- Empowered by insurance, families make informed decisions and unlock new opportunities without fear of setbacks.

Benefits of Networking and Community

Networking and community play a crucial role in maintaining a millionaire mindset and achieving financial freedom. Here's how these elements contribute to financial success:

Access to Knowledge and Information:

- **Learning from Others**: Networking with financially successful individuals provides access to their knowledge, experiences, and strategies. This can help you avoid common pitfalls and adopt best practices.
- **Staying Informed**: Being part of a community keeps you updated on market trends, investment opportunities, and financial strategies.

Opportunities for Collaboration and Partnerships:

- **Business Ventures**: Networking can lead to partnerships in business ventures or investment opportunities that you might not have discovered on your own.

- **Joint Ventures**: Collaborating with others can pool resources, reduce risks, and enhance the potential for success in various projects.

Motivation and Accountability:

- **Support System**: Being part of a community provides emotional support and encouragement, which is essential for staying motivated.
- **Accountability**: Sharing your financial goals with a network can create a sense of accountability, as peers can encourage you to stay on track and celebrate your successes.

Exposure to Different Perspectives:

- **Diverse Insights**: Interacting with individuals from different backgrounds and industries exposes you to a variety of perspectives and ideas, fostering innovative thinking and problem-solving.
- **Challenge Your Assumptions**: Engaging with others can challenge your preconceived

notions and encourage you to consider new approaches to financial growth.

Building Confidence and Reducing Isolation:

- **Confidence Boost**: Success stories and positive reinforcement from your network can boost your confidence in your ability to achieve financial goals.
- **Reducing Isolation**: Financial journeys can be isolating. Being part of a community helps you feel connected and supported.

How to Build and Leverage Your Network and Community

1. **Join Professional Organizations and Associations**:
    - ➢ Become a member of professional groups related to your industry or financial interests. These organizations often provide networking events, educational resources, and opportunities for collaboration. Ex. The Independent Financial Professionals Association (IFPA)

2. **Attend Conferences and Seminars**:
   - Participate in industry conferences, seminars, and workshops. These events are great for meeting like-minded individuals and learning from experts. Ex. Annual meets/Monthly meets by Foundation of Independent Financial Associates (FIFA)

3. **Utilize Social Media and Online Platforms**:
   - Engage in online communities, forums, and social media groups focused on financial independence and wealth-building. Platforms like LinkedIn, Reddit, and Facebook have groups dedicated to these topics.

4. **Engage in Local Networking Events**:
   - Attend local meetups, business networking events, and community gatherings. Building local connections can be beneficial for forming more personal and direct relationships. Ex. BNI (Business Network International) local events.

5. **Find a Mentor or Become One**:
   - o Seek out mentors who can provide guidance, advice, and support based on their experiences. Similarly, mentoring others can reinforce your own knowledge and expand your network. Ex. Tony Robbins.

6. **Join Investment Clubs**:
   - o Participate in investment clubs where members pool their resources and share investment strategies. This collaborative approach can enhance your financial knowledge and investment skills.

7. **Participate in Mastermind Groups**:
   - o Join or form mastermind groups with individuals who share similar financial goals. These groups meet regularly to discuss goals, share insights, and provide mutual support.

8. **Volunteer and Give Back**:
   - o Engage in community service and volunteer work. Giving back not only feels rewarding but also connects

you with others who value making a positive impact, which can lead to valuable relationships.

Example of How to Use Networking and Community

Imagine you're aiming to achieve early financial freedom. You decide to join a local professional association for entrepreneurs and attend their monthly meetings. At one meeting, you meet a successful business owner who shares their story of how they achieved financial freedom by investing in real estate. Inspired, you ask if they'd be willing to mentor you. Over time, this mentorship provides you with valuable insights and guidance on real estate investing.

Simultaneously, you join an online community focused on financial independence. Through this platform, you learn about different investment strategies, stay updated on market trends, and receive advice from others who are on a similar journey. You also participate in discussions and share your own experiences, helping others and reinforcing your own knowledge.

As you progress, you attend a few industry conferences where you connect with potential business partners. These new relationships lead to joint ventures that further accelerate your path to financial freedom. The support and accountability from your network keep you motivated and focused on your goals.

By actively building and leveraging your network and community, you can gain valuable knowledge, discover new opportunities, and stay motivated on your journey to financial freedom. The collective wisdom and support from a strong network can significantly enhance your chances of success.

FOOD FOR THOUGHT

" A millionaire mindset isn't about having a million dollars, but about believing you can create it. "

Chapter 3: Understanding Financial Markets

Importance of Bank Accounts in Building an Economy

What is a Bank Account?

A bank account is a place where you can safely keep your money. You can put money into your account (deposit) and take money out (withdraw) whenever you need it. There are different types of bank accounts, such as checking accounts for everyday use and savings accounts to save money for the future.

1. **Safe Storage of Money**:
   - **For Individuals**: Bank accounts provide a safe place to store money, protecting it from theft or loss.
   - **For Businesses**: Companies can keep their earnings secure and manage their finances more effectively.
2. **Facilitates Transactions**:
   - **Convenient Payments**: People and businesses can pay for goods and

services electronically, which is faster and safer than using cash.

- o **Efficient Transfers**: Money can be easily transferred between accounts, both within the same country and internationally.

3. **Savings and Investments**:
   - o **Interest Earnings**: Savings accounts often earn interest, meaning the bank pays you a small amount of money for keeping your money with them.
   - o **Investment Opportunities**: Banks offer various investment products that can help individuals and businesses grow their wealth.

4. **Access to Credit**:
   - o **Loans**: Banks provide loans to individuals for things like buying a house or starting a business. This helps people achieve personal goals and stimulates economic activity.
   - o **Credit History**: Having a bank account and using it responsibly helps build a credit history, which is important for getting loans in the future.

5. **Economic Stability**:
   - **Monetary Policy**: Banks play a crucial role in a country's monetary policy by controlling the supply of money and interest rates. This helps manage inflation and ensure economic stability.
   - **Government Programs**: Banks help distribute government benefits and stimulus payments, ensuring that financial support reaches those in need.

6. **Encourages Saving and Financial Planning**:
   - **Budgeting**: With a bank account, individuals can better track their income and expenses, making it easier to budget and plan for the future.
   - **Emergency Funds**: Savings accounts help people set aside money for emergencies, reducing financial stress during unexpected situations.

7. **Promotes Economic Growth**:
   - **Business Expansion**: Access to banking services allows businesses to grow, create jobs, and contribute to economic development.

- o **Innovation and Entrepreneurship**: Banks support new ideas and startups by providing the necessary financial resources, fostering innovation and entrepreneurship.

Summary

In simple terms, bank accounts are essential for safely managing money, making payments, saving for the future, and accessing credit. They play a crucial role in promoting economic stability and growth by enabling efficient financial transactions, encouraging savings, and supporting businesses and individuals.

How safe are our money in bank accounts

In India, the safety of money in bank accounts is ensured through several measures involving regulatory frameworks, deposit insurance, and robust security practices. Here's an overview of how safe your money is in Indian bank accounts:

1. Regulation and Oversight

- **Reserve Bank of India (RBI)**: The RBI is the central banking authority in India, regulating and supervising all banks to ensure they adhere to strict guidelines and maintain financial stability. The RBI conducts regular audits and inspections of banks to monitor their health and performance.

- **Financial Stability**: Banks are required to maintain certain levels of capital adequacy and liquidity to ensure they can handle financial stress and meet their obligations.

2. Deposit Insurance

- **Deposit Insurance and Credit Guarantee Corporation (DICGC)**: In India, deposits are insured by the DICGC, a subsidiary of the RBI. This insurance covers deposits up to ₹5 lakh per depositor per bank. This means that in the unlikely event of a bank failure, each depositor is protected up to this limit.

3. Security Measures

- **Cybersecurity**: Indian banks implement advanced cybersecurity measures to protect against hacking and fraud. This includes encryption, secure login methods, and continuous monitoring of transactions for suspicious activity.

- **Physical Security**: Banks also employ strong physical security measures, such as vaults, surveillance cameras, and security personnel, to safeguard against physical theft.

4. Financial Stability Measures

- **Risk Management**: Banks in India adopt comprehensive risk management practices to minimize potential financial risks. This includes diversifying their investment portfolios and maintaining adequate capital reserves.
- **Access to Liquidity**: In times of financial distress, Indian banks have access to liquidity support from the RBI, which can provide funds to meet short-term needs and prevent liquidity crises.

5. Customer Protections

- **Fraud Protection**: Many Indian banks offer protection against unauthorized transactions. Customers are advised to report any suspicious activity immediately to benefit from such protections.
- **Dispute Resolution**: Banks have customer service and dispute resolution mechanisms

in place to address complaints and issues efficiently.

6. Legal Protections

- **Consumer Rights**: Indian banking laws protect consumers' rights, ensuring fair treatment and transparency. The Banking Ombudsman Scheme, operated by the RBI, provides a platform for consumers to resolve grievances with banks.
- **Transparency Requirements**: Banks must provide clear and accurate information about their products and services, helping customers make informed decisions.

Summary

Overall, money in Indian bank accounts is quite safe due to a combination of regulatory oversight by the RBI, deposit insurance through the DICGC, strong security practices, and legal protections for consumers. While no system can guarantee complete risk elimination, these measures significantly reduce the likelihood of losing money due to bank failures, fraud, or other financial risks.

Budgeting and Saving

What is Budgeting?

Budgeting is the process of creating a plan to manage your money. This plan outlines how you will spend your income, including paying for essentials, discretionary spending, and savings. It involves tracking your income and expenses to ensure you do not spend more than you earn.

Why We Need to Budget?

1. **Financial Control**:
   - **Prevents Overspending**: A budget helps you keep track of your spending, ensuring you do not spend more than you earn.
   - **Allocates Resources Wisely**: It allows you to prioritize your spending on essentials and savings before discretionary items.
2. **Achieve Financial Goals**:
   - **Savings Goals**: Whether it's saving for a vacation, a new car, or a down payment on a house, budgeting helps you set aside money systematically.
   - **Debt Repayment**: A budget can help you allocate funds to pay off debts,

reducing financial stress and improving your credit score.

3. **Emergency Preparedness**:
    o **Emergency Fund**: Budgeting allows you to build an emergency fund, which can cover unexpected expenses like medical bills or car repairs, providing a financial safety net.

4. **Improves Financial Awareness**:
    o **Understanding Spending Habits**: By tracking your spending, you become more aware of where your money goes and can identify areas where you might cut back.
    o **Informed Decisions**: Knowledge of your financial situation helps you make informed decisions about major purchases and investments.

What is Saving?

Saving is the act of setting aside a portion of your income for future use. This can be for short-term needs, like an upcoming purchase, or long-term goals, such as retirement. Savings are usually kept in a bank account or other secure places where they can earn interest over time.

Why We Need to Save?

1. **Financial Security**:
    - **Emergencies**: Having savings means you are better prepared to handle unexpected expenses, reducing the need for high-interest debt like credit cards or payday loans.
    - **Job Loss**: Savings can provide a buffer if you lose your job, giving you time to find a new one without immediate financial pressure.
2. **Achieving Life Goals**:
    - **Major Purchases**: Savings help you afford major purchases without needing to rely entirely on credit, such as buying a car or home.
    - **Education**: Saving for education can help cover tuition fees and other

associated costs, either for yourself or your children.

3. **Retirement Planning:**
   - o **Future Security**: Saving for retirement ensures you have funds to support yourself when you are no longer working, allowing for a comfortable lifestyle in your later years.
   - o **Compound Interest**: Starting to save early allows your money to grow through compound interest, significantly increasing your retirement funds over time.

4. **Avoiding Debt:**
   - o **Less Reliance on Credit**: Having savings reduces your reliance on borrowing, which can lead to high-interest debt.
   - o **Debt Repayment**: Savings can also help pay down existing debt faster, reducing overall interest payments and financial burden.

Summary

Budgeting and saving are essential practices for achieving financial stability and security. Budgeting helps you manage your income and expenses, ensuring you do not overspend and can allocate money toward savings and other financial goals. Saving provides a financial cushion for emergencies, enables you to achieve life goals, supports retirement planning, and helps you avoid debt. Together, these practices foster a sense of control over your financial future and reduce stress related to money matters.

Case Study - The spending trap: where does your money go?

Gadget Overload:
- Tempted by Trends: Technology companies churn out new "must-have" devices, fueling impulsive purchases that quickly lose their appeal.
- Cluttered Spaces: Unused gadgets accumulate, creating disorganization and wasted money.

Food on Demand:
- Convenience Comes at a Cost: Frequent online food orders add up, eating into savings.

- Unhealthy Habits: Relying on food delivery impacts health and budget.

Online Shopping Frenzy:
- Targeted Temptations: Social media bombards us with product recommendations, making overspending easy.
- Discount Deception: Enticing discounts trick us into unnecessary purchases.

The Savings Gap:
- Rising Incomes, Shrinking Savings: Despite earning more, small expenses erode savings.
- Prioritizing Needs over Wants: Instant gratification challenges long-term financial goals.

Taking Control - Financial Planning:
- Track Spending: Understand where your money goes using budgeting tools.
- Set Goals: Establish realistic financial objectives (e.g., down payment, emergency fund).

Empowering Your Financial Future:
- Achieve Your Dreams: Taking control unlocks freedom to pursue your goals.
- Financial Security: Effective planning protects against unexpected challenges.

Why is Inflation Important to Consider?
What is Inflation?

Inflation is the rate at which the general level of prices for goods and services rises, leading to a decrease in the purchasing power of money. In simpler terms, when inflation occurs, each unit of currency buys fewer goods and services than it did in the past. Inflation is typically measured annually and expressed as a percentage.

Considering inflation is crucial for several reasons:

1. **Erosion of Purchasing Power**:
   - **Cost of Living**: As prices rise, the same amount of money buys fewer goods and services. This means that over time, the cost-of-living increases, and people need more money to maintain the same standard of living.
   - **Savings Impact**: Inflation can erode the value of savings. Money saved today may have less purchasing power in the future if it does not grow at a rate that keeps up with inflation.

2. **Interest Rates and Borrowing**:
   - **Loan Costs**: Inflation affects interest rates. Central banks, like the Federal Reserve in the U.S. or the Reserve Bank of India, often adjust interest rates to control inflation. Higher interest rates make borrowing more expensive, which can impact mortgages, car loans, and business investments.
   - **Investment Returns**: Investors seek returns that outpace inflation. If inflation is high, the real returns on investments need to be higher to maintain purchasing power.

3. **Wages and Income**:
   - **Wage Adjustments**: In an inflationary environment, workers may demand higher wages to keep up with the rising cost of living. Businesses must then balance higher labor costs with their pricing strategies.
   - **Fixed Incomes**: People on fixed incomes, such as retirees with pensions, can struggle during periods

of high inflation if their income does not increase accordingly.

4. **Economic Planning and Policy**:
    o **Monetary Policy**: Central banks use tools like interest rate adjustments to control inflation. Understanding inflation trends helps in formulating effective monetary policies.
    o **Fiscal Policy**: Governments consider inflation when planning budgets, tax policies, and public spending. High inflation can lead to higher costs for government projects and services.

Historical Context: The Last 75 Years

Considering the last 75 years of data highlights several important trends and lessons about inflation:

1. **Post-War Inflation**: After World War II, many countries experienced significant inflation due to increased demand and rebuilding efforts. This period showed how economic recovery can drive prices up.
2. **1970s Inflation Surge**: The 1970s saw a period of high inflation, known as

stagflation, where high inflation was coupled with stagnant economic growth. This period underscored the complexities of managing inflation without hampering growth.

3. **Monetary Policy Evolution**: The late 20th century saw central banks around the world adopting more sophisticated monetary policies to control inflation. This included targeting specific inflation rates to stabilize economies.

4. **Globalization**: Increased globalization in recent decades has influenced inflation by affecting supply chains and production costs. While it has helped keep prices lower for many goods, disruptions can cause inflationary pressures.

5. **Recent Trends**: In the past few years, various factors like the COVID-19 pandemic, supply chain disruptions, and geopolitical tensions have led to significant inflation in many parts of the world. This highlights the importance of flexibility and responsiveness in economic policies.

Year	Inflation Rate (%)	Value of Money
1980	11	100000
1985	6.5	61866
1990	8.4	39618
1995	7.8	23595
2000	13.5	13798
2005	10.3	8329
2010	4.3	5784
2015	4.7	4361
2020	4.7	3522
2021	5.3	3335
2022	5.7	3145
2023	4.8	2994

Description:

The table presents a chronological summary of inflation rates and the corresponding value of money in India from 1980 to 2023. It shows how inflation has eroded the purchasing power of ₹100,000 over time.

- In 1980, ₹100,000 held full value, but by 1985, due to a 6.5% inflation rate, its value reduced to ₹61,866.

- By the year 2000, with inflation peaking at 13.5%, the value dropped further to ₹13,798.

- Despite a relatively lower inflation rate of around 4-5% in recent years, the value of

₹100,000 in 1980 terms was only ₹2,994 by 2023.

The data effectively highlights the long-term impact of inflation on money's purchasing power and serves as a powerful illustration of why investing and inflation-hedging strategies are critical for preserving wealth.

Summary

Inflation is a critical economic factor that impacts purchasing power, interest rates, wages, savings, and overall economic stability. Historical data over the last 75 years reveals the various ways inflation has influenced economies and underscores the importance of monitoring and managing it effectively. For individuals, understanding inflation helps in making informed decisions about spending, saving, and investing to protect and grow their financial well-being. For policymakers, it provides insights for designing effective monetary and fiscal policies to sustain economic health.

FOOD FOR THOUGHT

" *Financial markets are the language of wealth; mastering it is the key to unlocking your financial future.* "

Chapter 4: Emergency Funds

What is an Emergency Fund?

An **emergency fund** is a savings reserve set aside to cover unexpected expenses or financial emergencies. These can include situations like medical emergencies, car repairs, job loss, or urgent home repairs. The purpose of an emergency fund is to provide financial security and prevent the need to rely on high-interest debt, such as credit cards or loans, during unforeseen circumstances.

Why Do We Need an Emergency Fund?

1. **Financial Security**:
   - **Peace of Mind**: Knowing you have money set aside for emergencies reduces financial stress and anxiety.
   - **Independence**: It allows you to handle unexpected expenses without needing to borrow money from friends, family, or lenders.
2. **Avoiding Debt**:

- o **Preventing High-Interest Debt**: An emergency fund helps you avoid taking on high-interest debt, such as credit card debt or payday loans, which can be costly and difficult to pay off.
- o **Protecting Credit Score**: Using savings instead of credit preserves your credit score by avoiding late payments and high credit utilization.

3. **Job Security**:
   - o **Cushion for Job Loss**: In case of job loss, an emergency fund provides a financial cushion, giving you time to find new employment without immediate financial pressure.

4. **Unexpected Expenses**:
   - o **Handling Unexpected Costs**: Emergencies like medical bills, car repairs, or urgent home repairs can be covered without disrupting your regular budget.

5. **Flexibility and Opportunities**:
   - o **Career Changes**: An emergency fund can give you the flexibility to pursue new career opportunities or take

time off for personal reasons without immediate financial concerns.

The Layoff Landscape

1. Tech Sector Layoffs

In 2023, over 262,000 employees were laid off worldwide, affecting more than 1,180 tech firms, primarily in the United States.

2. Broader Economic Impact

Between August and December 2022, the U.S. experienced 6.9 million layoffs, with an additional 168,000 since the start of 2023.

3. Industry-Specific Trends

The trade and transportation sector saw 1.46 million layoffs from June 2021 to June 2022.

The Human Impact of Layoffs
- **Layoff Experience**

40% of Americans have experienced a job loss, a sobering statistic that highlights the widespread impact of layoffs.

- **Layoff Anxiety**

48% of people report feeling anxious about the prospect of being laid off, a testament to the emotional toll of economic uncertainty.

- **Recent Layoffs**

28% of Americans have been laid off within the past two years, underscoring the need for financial resilience.

- **The Human Face**

Behind the numbers are real people facing the stress, financial hardship, and personal challenges of job loss.

How Much Do We Need in an Emergency Fund?
The amount needed in an emergency fund can vary based on individual circumstances, but here are some general guidelines:

1. **Basic Recommendation:**
   - ➢ **6 to 12 Months of Expenses**: Financial experts typically recommend having enough to cover 6 to 12 months of essential living expenses. This includes rent or mortgage, utilities, groceries, transportation, insurance, and other necessary costs.

2. **Personal Factors to Consider:**
   - ➢ **Job Stability**: If you have a stable job with a steady income, 3 months of expenses might be sufficient. If your job is less secure or your income fluctuates, aim for 6 months or more.
   - ➢ **Dependents**: If you have dependents (children, elderly parents), you may need a larger emergency fund to account for their needs.
   - ➢ **Health**: If you have ongoing medical issues or high healthcare costs, consider setting aside additional funds.
   - ➢ **Debt Levels**: If you have significant debt, a larger emergency fund can help you manage debt payments during financial hardships.
   - ➢ **Lifestyle and Expenses**: Higher living expenses or a more expensive lifestyle require a larger emergency fund to maintain.

3. **Starting Small and Building Up**:
   ➢ **Initial Goal**: If saving 3 to 6 months of expenses seems daunting, start with a smaller goal, such as ₹5,000 or ₹10,000. Gradually build up your fund over time by consistently setting aside a portion of your income.

Summary

An **emergency fund** is a crucial financial safety net designed to cover unexpected expenses and provide financial stability during emergencies. It helps avoid high-interest debt, protects your credit score, and offers peace of mind. The general recommendation is to save enough to cover 6 to 12 months of essential living expenses, but individual needs may vary based on factors like job stability, dependents, health, debt levels, and lifestyle. Starting with a smaller amount and consistently saving can help you build a robust emergency fund over time.

Case Study - A Cautionary Tale of a Hotel Owner's Downfall

The Devastating Consequences of Poor Financial Planning: A Cautionary Tale of a Hotel Owner's Downfall

Poor Financial Planning:

- The hotel owner's poor financial planning led to bankruptcy and zero bank balance.

- Lack of advance payments from customers during lockdown further worsened the situation.

Financial Stability:

- The tragic tale emphasizes the need for a comprehensive financial plan.

- Setting aside emergency funds and diversifying income streams are essential for financial security.

Lessons Learned:

- The story serves as a reminder of the devastating consequences of not having a solid financial strategy in place.

- It highlights the importance of managing finances effectively for stability during crises.

FOOD FOR THOUGHT

" An emergency fund is like a parachute: you hope you'll never need it, but you're awfully glad you have it when you do."

Chapter 5: Mastering Debt Management and Credit Health

What is debt?

Debt refers to borrowed money that must be repaid, typically with interest.

How Loans Work?

- ➢ **Components of a Loan:**
  - ▪ **Principal**: The borrowed amount.
  - ▪ **Interest Rate**: The cost of borrowing.
  - ▪ **Tenure**: Duration for repayment.
- ➢ **Application Process:**
  - ▪ Apply to a bank or trusted NBFC.
  - ▪ Lenders assess income, credit score, and debt levels.
  - ▪ If approved, funds are disbursed.
- ➢ **Repayment:**
  - ▪ Regular installments until the loan is paid off
- ➢ **Individual Insolvency:**
  - ▪ If someone faces debt issues, they can initiate insolvency proceedings.

- Under the **Insolvency and Bankruptcy Code, 2016 (IBC)**, both creditors and debtors can file for individual insolvency.
- The court appoints an interim receiver to manage the debtor's assets.
- The IBC provides a fresh start regime for debtors.

Secured Loans vs Unsecured Loans

Let me explain the difference between secured loans and unsecured loans:

1. **Secured Loans:**
   - **Collateral**: Secured loans require collateral, which is an asset you pledge to the lender (e.g., your car, home, or investment account).
   - **Risk and Benefit**: By providing collateral, you reduce the lender's risk. If you fail to repay the loan, the lender can seize the collateral.
   - **Examples**: Home loans (mortgages) and auto loans are common secured loans.
   - **Interest Rates**: Typically, secured loans have lower interest rates compared to unsecured loans.

2. Unsecured Loans:

- ➢ **No Collateral**: Unsecured loans don't require collateral. Lenders evaluate your creditworthiness based on factors like credit history, income, and outstanding debts.
- ➢ **Risk and Benefit**: While you won't risk losing an asset, unsecured loans may have higher interest rates due to the lack of collateral.
- ▪ **Examples**: Personal loans, credit cards, and student loans fall under this category.
- ▪ **Qualification**: To get the best offer, you'll need a strong credit score and solid finances.

Remember, both types have their pros and cons, so choose wisely based on your needs and financial situation!

Good Debt vs Bad Debt

1. Good Debt:

- ➢ **Purpose**: Good debt is incurred for investments or assets that can potentially appreciate or generate income.
- ▪ **Examples**:
  - ▪ **Education Loans**: Investing in education can lead to better career prospects and higher earning potential.

- **Home Loans**: Buying a home is an investment that appreciates over time.
    - **Business Loans**: Funding a business venture can yield returns.

- ➤ **Benefit**: Good debt contributes positively to your financial well-being.

2. **Bad Debt**:

- ➤ **Purpose**: Bad debt arises from unnecessary or frivolous spending.
- **Examples**:
    - **Credit Card Debt**: Accumulating high-interest debt for non-essential purchases.
    - **Consumer Loans**: Borrowing for luxury items or vacations.

- ➤ **Risk**: Bad debt drains your finances without adding value.

Remember, managing debt wisely is essential for financial stability!

Credit management and CIBIL score

Let's explore **credit management** and the factors that influence your **CIBIL score** in India:

Credit Management:

- **Definition**: Credit management involves processes related to granting credit, setting terms, recovering payments, and ensuring compliance with credit policies.
- **Purpose**: It helps protect your business from late payments, defaults, and bad debts.
- **Benefits**:

  - **Cash Flow Protection**: Ensures positive cash inflows for timely bill payments and employee salaries.
  - **Reduced Late Payments**: Detects late payments early, preventing defaults.
  - **Increased Liquidity**: Improves available business liquidity.
  - **Debt Recovery**: Facilitates faster and more complete debt recovery.
  - **Days Sales Outstanding (DSO) Improvement**: Reduces the time it takes to collect payments.
  - **Strategic Planning**: Helps analyze performance and prepare financial budgets.
  - **Lender Confidence**: Reassures potential lenders for business expansion.

CIBIL Score

Definition: The CIBIL Score, also known as the Credit Score, is a numerical summary of a consumer's credit history and a reflection of the person's credit profile. It ranges from 300 to 900, with 900 being the best score possible.

Purpose: The purpose of the CIBIL Score in India is to help lenders determine the risk of lending money to a consumer. A higher CIBIL Score indicates a higher chance of the loan being repaid on time, thus making the individual a less risky borrower. It's used by banks and financial institutions to evaluate and approve loans and credit card applications.

Factors Influencing CIBIL Score:

- **Payment History** (35% weightage):
  - Timeliness of loan repayments and credit card payments.
  - Instances of defaults, late payments, or delinquencies.
- **Credit Utilization**:
  - Proportion of available credit currently used.
- **Credit Mix**:
  - Types of credit (secured or unsecured).
    - **Multiple Inquiries:**

- Frequent credit inquiries negatively impact the score.
  - **Length of Credit History**:
- Longer credit history is favorable.

Remember, maintaining a healthy credit score is crucial for financial stability!

Leverage and Debt Management for Wealth Creation

Understanding Leverage

Leverage, in financial terms, refers to using borrowed capital to increase the potential return on investment. In India, leverage can be a powerful tool for wealth creation when used wisely.

How to Use Leverage?

1. Real Estate Investing

 - Use home loans to purchase property with a down payment of 10-20%.

 - Example: Purchase a ₹1 crore property with a ₹20 lakh down payment and ₹80 lakh loan.

2. Business Expansion

 - Utilize business loans to grow your enterprise.

- Example: Borrow ₹50 lakh to open a new store that generates ₹1 crore in annual revenue.

3. Margin Trading
- Use margin funding from brokers to invest more in stocks.
- Example: Invest ₹1 lakh of your money and borrow ₹1 lakh to purchase ₹2 lakh worth of shares.

4. Education Loans
- Invest in your skills and knowledge to increase earning potential.
- Example: Take a ₹10 lakh education loan for an MBA, potentially doubling your salary.

5. Credit Card Rewards
- Use credit cards for planned expenses to earn rewards, but pay full balance.
- Example: Earn 2% cashback on ₹50,000 monthly spending, gaining ₹12,000 annually.

Importance in Debt Management and Wealth Creation

1. Accelerated Wealth Accumulation
- Control larger assets with less capital.

- Example: ₹20 lakh down payment controls a ₹1 crore property, benefiting from its full appreciation.

2. Tax Benefits

- Claim deductions on home loan interest (up to ₹2 lakh annually) and principal repayment (under Section 80C).
- Education loan interest is fully deductible under Section 80E.

3. Inflation Hedge

- Fixed-rate loans become easier to repay over time as the rupee's value decreases.
- Example: A ₹50 lakh loan today might feel like ₹30 lakh in purchasing power after 10 years of 5% inflation.

4. Cash Flow Management

- Make large investments without depleting savings.
- Example: Start a business with a ₹25 lakh loan while keeping your ₹10 lakh savings as emergency fund.

Risk Management

1. Maintain a Healthy Debt-to-Income Ratio

- Keep total EMIs below 40% of monthly income.

- Example: If monthly income is ₹1 lakh, limit total EMIs to ₹40,000.

2. Understand Loan Terms

- Compare interest rates, processing fees, and prepayment penalties across lenders.
- Example: A home loan at 8.5% p.a. from SBI might be better than 9% p.a. from a private bank.

3. Create an Emergency Fund

- Maintain 6-12 months of expenses in liquid savings.
- Example: If monthly expenses are ₹50,000, aim for ₹3-6 lakh in emergency fund.

4. Diversify Leveraged Investments

- Don't put all borrowed money in one asset or sector.
- Example: If borrowing ₹50 lakh, invest ₹30 lakh in real estate and ₹20 lakh in business expansion.

5. Insurance Coverage

- Protect leveraged assets with adequate insurance.
- Example: Get term life insurance of at least 10 times your annual income if you have dependents.

By applying these strategies and maintaining a balanced approach to leverage, individuals can potentially accelerate their wealth creation while managing the associated risks effectively.

Smart Money Moves: Loan Pre-Closure vs. Lump Sum Mutual Fund Investment

Let's break down the comparison between pre-closing a ₹10 lakh home loan or investing the same amount in mutual funds with a 15% Compound Annual Growth Rate (CAGR) over 20 years.

Below is a comparative table outlining key aspects of both strategies—pre-closing the loan versus investing the lump sum in mutual funds—and some additional points you might consider.

Parameter	Loan Pre-Closure	Lump Sum Mutual Fund Investment
Principal Amount	₹10,00,000	₹10,00,000
Interest Rate / Expected Return	10% per annum (Home Loan)	15% per annum (CAGR for Mutual Funds)
Tenure	20 years	20 years

Parameter	Loan Pre-Closure	Lump Sum Mutual Fund Investment
Monthly EMI (if not closed)	₹9,650	Not applicable
Total Amount Payable (if kept for 20 years)	₹23,16,052	Not applicable
Total Interest Paid (if kept for 20 years)	₹13,16,052	None (but there is an opportunity cost)
Future Value After 20 Years	Not applicable (Loan is closed early)	Approximately ₹1.64 crore (assuming 15% CAGR)
Pros	- Immediate interest savings by closing loan early- Psychological relief from being debt-free- Eliminates future rate	- Potentially higher long-term returns (15% CAGR)- Lump sum benefits from compounding over 20 years- Can meet long-

Parameter	Loan Pre-Closure	Lump Sum Mutual Fund Investment
	fluctuations (if interest rates rise)	term goals (e.g., retirement, wealth creation)
Cons	- Opportunity cost: The lump sum could have earned higher returns elsewhere- Potential loss of tax benefits on home loan interest (if you are availing them)- Reduced liquidity (money is locked into prepayment)	- Market timing risk (lump sum investment at market peak)- Emotional toll due to market volatility- No guaranteed returns, equity investments carry risk
Tax Implications	- Losing home loan interest tax deductions	- Long-term capital gains tax on equity funds

Parameter	Loan Pre-Closure	Lump Sum Mutual Fund Investment
	(Section 24, up to certain limits)- Must ensure no prepayment penalties on the loan	(after 1 year, 10% on gains above ₹1 lakh)- Tax planning can optimize returns
Impact on Monthly Cash Flow	- EMI outflow disappears if loan is closed, freeing up monthly cash- Improves monthly budget	- No immediate change in monthly outflow (assuming this was a surplus lump sum)- Potential growth in investment can improve future cash flow
Liquidity	- After pre-closure, funds are locked into the property	- Investments in mutual funds can be redeemed

Parameter	Loan Pre-Closure	Lump Sum Mutual Fund Investment
	(less liquid)- Home equity can be accessed only via loan against property or resale	partially or fully (subject to exit load or capital gains tax)- Greater liquidity if planned properly
Risk Considerations	- Minimal risk once the loan is closed (no interest rate or market risk)	- Subject to market fluctuations- Requires a higher risk tolerance
Psychological/ Emotional Aspect	- Relief from debt burden- better peace of mind	- Market fluctuations can cause stress- Requires discipline to stay invested long-term
Decision Pointers	- If you prefer guaranteed savings and	- If you have a higher risk appetite and a

Parameter	Loan Pre-Closure	Lump Sum Mutual Fund Investment
	psychological relief, consider pre-closure- Evaluate foregone tax benefits before closing the loan	long investment horizon, lump sum investment may yield better returns- Market valuations and personal financial goals should guide the timing

Final Thoughts

- **Blend Approach**: Some choose to partially prepay the loan (reducing EMI or tenure) and invest the remainder in mutual funds.

- **Opportunity Cost vs. Interest Savings**: Compare the guaranteed interest savings from early loan closure with the potential (but not guaranteed) market returns.

- **Personal Factors**: Risk tolerance, liquidity needs, and emotional comfort with debt are crucial in making the final decision.

Remember, personalized advice from a financial advisor is crucial.

Debt Repayment Strategies
Home Loan Interest Free
How to make your home loan interest free?

Let's break this down step by step:

1. **Home Loan Details:**

    Loan Amount: ₹50 lakhs

    Interest Rate: 10% per annum

    Loan Tenure: 20 years

    Home Loan EMI: 48,251 / month

2. **Total Repayment Amount:**

    Total repayment over 20 years = EMI × Number of Months

    Total repayment = ₹48,251 × 240 = ₹1,15,80,260

    Total Interest = 65,80,260

3. **Mutual Fund Details:**

> Expected CAGR (Compound Annual Growth Rate): 15%
>
> Investment Duration: 20 years
>
> Expected Amount: Rs. 65,18,606 (65.2 Lakhs)

4. **Investment Required:** To generate the wealth equivalent to your total interest payment from your mutual funds, you need to invest approximately **₹4,300 per month** in your mutual funds over 20 years, assuming a 15% CAGR.

Home Loan Free Strategy 1

How to make your home loan completely free?

Let's break this down step by step:

1. **Home Loan Details:**

> Loan Amount: ₹50 lakhs
> Interest Rate: 10% per annum
> Loan Tenure: 20 years
> Home Loan EMI: 48,251 / month

2. **Total Repayment Amount:**

Total repayment over 20 years = EMI × Number of Months

Total repayment = ₹48,251 × 240 = ₹1,15,80,260

3. **Mutual Fund Details:**

Expected CAGR (Compound Annual Growth Rate): 15%

Investment Duration: 20 years

Expected Amount: Rs. 1,21,27640 (1.2 Crores)

4. **Investment Required:**

To generate the wealth equivalent to your total interest payment from your mutual funds, you need to invest approximately **₹8,000 per month** in your mutual funds over 20 years, assuming a 15% CAGR.

Home Loan Free Strategy 2

How to make your home loan completely free without investing any additional money?

Increase the loan tenure and reduce the EMI amount. Invest the remaining amount (previous EMI - current EMI) into mutual funds

Let's break this down step by step:

1. **Home Loan Details:**

   Loan Amount: ₹50 lakhs

   Interest Rate: 10% per annum

   Loan Tenure: 30 years

   Home Loan EMI: 43,879 / month

2. **Total Repayment Amount:**

   Total repayment over 30 years = EMI × Number of Months

   Total repayment = ₹43,879 × 240 = ₹1,57,96,288

   Total Interest = 1,07,96,288

3. **Mutual Fund Details:**

   Expected CAGR (Compound Annual Growth Rate): 15%

   Investment Duration: 20 years

Expected Amount: Rs. 3,06,46936 (3.1 Crores)

4. **Investment Required:**

Now you can invest approximately **₹4,372 per month** in your mutual funds over 30 years, assuming a 15% CAGR. You will get **3.1 INR Crore** at the end of 30 years

Remember that these calculations are based on historical data and assumptions. Actual returns may vary. And mutual fund returns are subject to market fluctuations, so it's essential to review our investments periodically and adjust as needed. Consult a financial advisor for personalized advice.

FOOD FOR THOUGHT

" Debt can be a financial prison or a stepping stone to freedom. The key lies in understanding how to use it wisely."

Chapter 6: Different Income Types

In simple terms, income is the money that an individual or business receives in exchange for providing a good or service or through investing capital. It's essentially the earnings that are received over a period can come from various sources such as work (salary), renting out property, or investments (dividends). It's what allows individuals and businesses to sustain themselves, save, and invest for the future.

Income can generally be categorized into two main types - Active Income and Passive Income

What is Active Income?
Active income refers to earnings received from performing a service. This includes wages, tips, salaries, commissions, and income from businesses in which there is material participation. In simpler terms, it's the money you make from working directly, like the paycheck from your day job or profits from a business you run. It requires your time and effort to earn this income.

How can I increase my active income?

To increase your active income, consider the following strategies:

1. **Improve Skills**: Enhance your skills or learn new ones to qualify for higher-paying jobs or promotions.
2. **Education**: Invest in further education or certifications that can lead to better job opportunities.
3. **Side Hustle**: Start a side business or freelance based on your skills and interests.
4. **Negotiate Salary**: If you're employed, negotiate your salary or seek better-paying job positions.
5. **Efficiency**: Increase your efficiency to take on more work or higher-paying projects.

Remember, increasing active income often requires investing time and effort to see results.

What are some side hustle ideas?
Here are some side hustle ideas you might consider:

1. **Freelancing**: Offer your professional services on platforms like Upwork or Fiverr.
2. **Tutoring**: Teach subjects you're knowledgeable in or languages you're fluent in.
3. **Crafts and Handmade Goods**: Sell your crafts on Etsy or at local markets.
4. **Consulting**: Use your expertise to consult for businesses or individuals.
5. **Content Creation**: Start a blog, YouTube channel, or podcast on topics you're passionate about.

Choose something that aligns with your skills and interests for the best chance of success!

What is Passive Income?

Passive income is money earned with little to no daily effort to maintain it. It's often called "earning money while you sleep." Unlike active income, where you trade time for money (like a job), passive income is generated from activities or investments that don't require your active involvement after the initial effort. Examples include:

- **Rental income**: Money received from renting out property.

- **Dividends**: Money paid to shareholders from a company's profits.
- **Interest**: Earnings from lending money or depositing funds in interest-bearing accounts.
- **Royalties**: Payments for the use of your work, like a book or music.

The key idea is that passive income streams allow you to earn money without having to work actively for it on a regular basis.

How can I create passive income streams?

Creating passive income streams often requires an initial investment of time, money, or both, but can lead to earnings that require little ongoing effort. Here are some ways to create passive income:

1. **Invest in Dividend Stocks**: Buy shares in companies that pay out dividends regularly.
2. **Rental Properties**: Purchase property to rent out. This can provide a steady monthly income.
3. **Peer-to-Peer Lending**: Lend money through platforms and earn interest as passive income.

4. **Create an App or Software**: If you have a tech background, creating a digital product can generate ongoing sales.
5. **Invest in Bonds or CDs**: These fixed-income investments pay interest over time.
6. **Start a Blog or YouTube Channel**: With enough viewers, you can earn through ads, sponsorships, and affiliate marketing.
7. **Automate a Business**: If you own a business, automating processes can reduce your active involvement and create more passive earnings.

Remember, it's important to research and consider the potential risks and returns of each option before investing your resources.

Here are some passive income ideas that typically require little to no investment capital

1. **Affiliate Marketing**: Promote products or services and earn a commission for each sale through your affiliate link.
2. **Advertising Revenue**: Monetize your blog, website, or YouTube channel with ads.
3. **Create an Online Course**: If you have expertise in a subject, create a course and sell it on platforms like Udemy or Teachable.

4. **Write an eBook**: Self-publish an eBook on platforms like Amazon Kindle Direct Publishing.
5. **Rent Out Your Stuff**: Rent out items you own, like camera equipment or musical instruments, on peer-to-peer rental platforms.

Remember, while these may not require upfront capital, they do require time and effort to set up and maintain.

Insurance Advisor Role

As an insurance advisor, you typically don't need investment capital to start, since you're not purchasing inventory or investing in assets. Your income would come from commissions on the policies you sell.

Income from an insurance advisor role can be both active and passive:

- **Active Income**: When you are actively selling insurance policies and directly engaging with clients, the commissions you earn are considered active income because they are the result of your direct efforts.
- **Passive Income**: If you receive ongoing commissions from the renewal of policies

you've sold in the past, this can be considered passive income, as it doesn't require active work at the time the income is received.

So, while the initial commission is active, subsequent renewals can provide a source of passive income.

Case Study - Financial Planning through the Lens of Mumbai's Dabbawalas

In the heart of Mumbai, India, a network of lunch delivery men known as Dabbawalas have become an iconic symbol of efficiency. Dating back to the 1890s, these men, dressed in white and sporting traditional caps, ensure hundreds of thousands of home-cooked meals reach their destination daily.

The Dabbawalas operate a complex yet elegant system. They collect metal tiffin boxes (dabbas) from homes, meticulously sort them based on a network of symbols and colors. Without relying on any fancy technology, they navigate the city's busy streets using bicycles and trains, ensuring each lunchbox reaches the intended office worker. The key to their success lies in their remarkable teamwork and the ability to adapt their routes and plans around the ever-changing urban landscape.

Financial planning is just like that system. It helps you manage your money efficiently, just like the Dabbawalas manage their deliveries. You set a clear plan (like their delivery route), track your income and expenses (like they sort the lunchboxes), and adapt to life's changes (like they navigate around traffic). With a financial plan, you can achieve your goals, just like every lunchbox reaches its destination.

FOOD FOR THOUGHT

" Passive income is the secret ingredient to financial freedom, working its magic even when you're not."

Chapter 7 – Insurance

What is Insurance?

Insurance is a contract represented by a policy in which an individual or entity receives financial protection or reimbursement against losses from an insurance company. The company pools clients' risks to make payments more affordable for the insured.

Types of Insurance

- **Life Insurance:** Provides a monetary benefit to a decedent's family or other designated beneficiary.
- **Health Insurance:** Covers medical expenses.
- **Auto Insurance:** Protects against financial loss in the event of an accident or theft.
- **Property Insurance:** Covers damage to or loss of property.
- **Liability Insurance:** Protects against legal liabilities.

Benefits

- **Financial Security:** Offers peace of mind by reducing financial stress during unexpected events.
- **Risk Management:** Helps manage risk and provides a safety net.
- **Investment Opportunity:** Some policies like life insurance can act as an investment and help in wealth creation.

IRDAI

The regulatory authority for insurance in India is the **Insurance Regulatory and Development Authority of India (IRDAI)**. It oversees the insurance industry in India, ensuring that the laws and regulations are followed to protect policyholder interests.

The functions of IRDAI include:

- Regulating and promoting the insurance industry
- Protecting policyholder interests
- Ensuring the solvency of insurance providers
- Establishing guidelines for insurance products and practices

- Licensing and regulating insurance intermediaries
- Promoting transparency and fair practices

Various Channels that sell insurance products

There are two main categories of channels selling insurance products in India: direct channels and intermediary channels.

Direct Channels

➢ **Company Website and App:** Insurance companies allow customers to directly purchase and manage their policies online. This channel is convenient and transparent, but may not be suitable for everyone, especially those who need guidance in choosing the right plan.

➢ **Telemarketing:** This channel involves contacting potential customers by phone to sell them insurance products. It can be a good way to reach a wide audience, but it can also be intrusive.

Intermediary Channels

➢ **Insurance Agents:** Agents are licensed professionals who represent one or more insurance companies. They can provide personalized advice and help customers choose the right insurance plan.

➢ **Brokers:** Brokers are independent advisors who work with multiple insurance companies. They can compare plans from different insurers and find the best coverage for their clients.

➢ **Bancassurance:** This is a partnership between banks and insurance companies, where banks sell insurance products to their customers. This channel is convenient for customers who already trust their bank, but the selection of plans may be limited.

➢ **Micro-insurance Agents:** These agents sell small, affordable insurance policies to low-income customers in rural and urban areas.

➢ **Common Service Centers (CSCs):** These are government-run outlets that provide various services, including the sale of insurance products.

➢ **Web Aggregators:** These are online platforms that allow customers to compare insurance plans from different companies.

➢ **Insurance Marketing Firms (IMFs):** These are companies that specialize in selling insurance products. They may employ their own agents or partner with other distribution channels.

> **Point of Sale (POS):** This channel involves selling insurance products at retail outlets, such as car dealerships or electronics stores.

The choice of distribution channel depends on the customer's needs and preferences. Some customers may prefer the personalized advice of an agent, while others may prefer the convenience of buying online.

Why do we need different channels?

Current Statistics

India's insurance penetration, which is the total premium as a percentage of GDP, is still relatively low compared to developed economies. As of FY 2022-23 [Insurance Sector in India: Industry Overview, Market Size & Trends - IBEF], it stands at around 4% with a breakdown of:

- **Life Insurance:** Contributing around 3% to the total penetration. This translates to a slightly higher penetration rate than the global average and double that of emerging markets.
- **Non-Life Insurance:** Makes up the remaining 1% of the penetration rate. This segment is

experiencing growth, but still lags life insurance.

Here are some additional points to consider:

- **Growth Trends:** While the overall penetration rate is low, it has been steadily increasing in recent years. The life insurance sector has shown more significant growth compared to non-life.
- **Global Comparison:** India's insurance penetration is lower than developed economies but is at par or slightly above some emerging markets.

Different channels are promoted for the following reasons.

- **Reach a wider audience**: Different channels allow insurers to reach various segments of the market, including those who may not be accessible through traditional means.
- **Cater to customer preferences**: Some customers prefer personal interaction with agents, while others might choose the convenience of online platforms.
- **Leverage specialized expertise**: Brokers and corporate agents often have specialized

knowledge that can help tailor insurance products to specific customer needs.

- **Increase accessibility**: Channels like common service centers and bancassurance make it easier for customers in remote areas or those who frequent banks to access insurance products.
- **Diversify marketing strategies**: Using multiple channels helps insurers mitigate risks and not rely on a single source for sales.

Each channel has its strengths and caters to different customer needs and buying behaviors.

How can we make Term Insurance free from Premiums?

Below is a detailed comparison table outlining both options with additional insights on how smart planning can essentially make your term insurance "free" by offsetting higher premium costs through investment gains:

Parameter	Option 1 (Shorter Premium Term)	Option 2 (Extended Premium Term + Investment of Difference)

Policy Coverage	₹2 Crore	₹2 Crore
Age	35	35
Policy Term	25 years (until age 60)	25 years (until age 60)
Premium Payment Term	5 years	25 years
Annual Premium	₹95,000	₹30,000
Total Premium Paid	₹95,000 x 5 = ₹4,75,000	₹30,000 x 25 = ₹7,50,000
Extra Cash Flow per Year (for 5 years)	–	₹95,000 – ₹30,000 = ₹65,000 (available for investment annually for the first 5 years)
Total Extra Investment	–	₹65,000 x 5 ≈ ₹3,24,600
Investment Assumption	–	Invested in Mutual Funds at an assumed 12% CAGR
Expected Future Value	–	Approximately ₹19,54,486

of Extra Investment		after the investment horizon*
Net Wealth Gain from Investment	–	Approx. ₹16,34,000 (calculated as the difference between the future value and the total extra invested amount)
Key Advantages	- Lower total outflow over a short period- Immediate relief from future premium payments- Simplified budgeting for a 5-year commitment	- Lower annual premium improves short-term cash flow- Investment of the premium difference generates significant wealth- Can offset the higher cumulative

		premium cost over 25 years
Key Considerations	- Requires a larger annual premium commitment for only 5 years- No additional wealth creation beyond premium savings	- Long-term premium commitment (25 years)- Involves market risk with the mutual fund investment- Requires discipline to invest the extra funds consistently over the initial 5 years
Overall Concept	You pay a higher premium for a limited period, and once paid, you're fully covered without	By paying a lower premium over a longer term and investing the difference, the investment gains can effectively

	future premium outlays.	"cover" or offset the cost of insurance— making it nearly cost-neutral over time

*Note: The expected future value and wealth gain assume of a 12% CAGR on the extra invested amount over the designated period.

Final Thoughts

Option 2 demonstrates a smart trick: by reducing your annual premium outlay and investing in the difference, you can create a substantial wealth gain that may effectively cover the cost of the term insurance. This approach leverages the power of compounding to offset higher premium costs, potentially making your term insurance "free" in terms of net cost. The decision will ultimately depend on your risk tolerance, discipline in investing, and long-term financial goals.

Remember that these calculations are based on historical data and assumptions. Actual returns may vary. And mutual fund returns are subject to market fluctuations, so it's essential to review our investments periodically and adjust as needed. Consult a financial advisor for personalized advice.

Medical Inflation in India

Medical inflation in India is projected to hit 11% in 2026, up from 9.6% in 2023, as healthcare costs are expected to exceed pre-pandemic levels. Another report suggests an alarming medical inflation rate of 14% post covid.

Why is medical inflation so high?

Medical inflation in India is high due to several factors:

- Increased demand for healthcare services.
- Advancements in medical technology which often come at a higher cost.
- Rising costs of raw materials and medicines.
- Higher wages for medical staff.
- Increased healthcare access and new treatments

Key Points about Medical Inflation in India

1. High Inflation Rate:
  - India has one of the highest medical inflation rates in Asia, reaching 14%.

2. Financial Burden on Employees:
  - 71% of employees personally cover their healthcare expenses.
  - Healthcare costs exceed 10% of total expenditure for over 90 million individuals.

3. Employer-Supported Health Insurance:
  - Only 15% of India's workforce receives health insurance support from their employers.
  - There is a significant disparity in the adoption of employer-sponsored healthcare plans, with younger employees (aged 20-30) adopting at half the rate of older employees (aged 51 and above).

4. Desire for Customizable Healthcare Plans:
  - 42% of employees desire "flex benefits," which allow them to customize their healthcare plans.

5. Lack of Comprehensive Healthcare Support:
  - Only 12% of companies provide telehealth support, and less than 1% offer outpatient coverage.

- 85% of employees with chronic illnesses do not feel supported by their employers.

6. Preventive Health Measures:
- Nearly 59% of employees skip their annual health checkups.
- 90% neglect regular consultations to monitor their health.

7. Strategic Investment in Employee Health:
- Investing in employee health goes beyond providing health insurance and includes preventive measures and comprehensive healthcare options.

These key points highlight the significant challenges and gaps in healthcare support for employees in India and underscore the need for strategic investments in employee health and well-being.

How Hospitals Charge 25% More for Those Without Insurance: The Shocking Truth

Insurance Impact on Hospital Bills:

- Self-paying patients at some leading hospitals are charged higher rates than those with insurance, leading to a 27% increase in bills.

- These pricing practices are not publicly disclosed.

Patient Experience:

- A patient at a leading Hospital, Gurgaon experienced a significant bill increase due to lack of insurance coverage, highlighting the cost disparity for self-paying patients.

Billing Differences:

- A comparative analysis shows that hospital charges vary greatly between insured and uninsured patients, especially in consultation fees, investigations, and room rents.

Industry and Doctor Opinions:

- Some industry experts criticize the higher charges for self-paying patients as unjust and potentially exploitative.
- Insurers negotiate lower rates with hospitals, benefiting insured patients.

Customer vs. Patient Treatment:

- Insured individuals benefit from discounted rates due to hospital-insurer partnerships.

- Uninsured patients may be charged higher rates without such negotiations.

This case study stresses the importance of proper health insurance coverage.

The 5th Tyre: Why You Need Insurance?

Imagine you're buying a new car. How many tyres do you think it will have? Most people would say four, right? But here's an interesting twist: there's actually a fifth tyre—the spare tyre. We don't need it for everyday driving, but it's there just in case.

Now, let's draw a parallel to insurance. Consider yourself as the breadwinner of your family. If something happens to you, could your family survive financially for six months without your income? It's a tough situation, isn't it? That's where term insurance comes in. By getting a term insurance policy with coverage of at least 2 crores, you're ensuring your family's financial stability even if you're not around.

But wait, there's more! Just like that spare tyre, health insurance is crucial too. Imagine a scenario where you or a family member faces a serious health issue and needs hospitalization. Without health insurance, the burden of medical bills can be overwhelming. So, having both health and term insurance is essential.

Remember, medical costs are rising—especially after COVID-19. Don't delay; make an informed decision today. Your family's well-being depends on it!"

How to become an IRDA certified insurance advisor in India?

There are three main steps to become an IRDA certified insurance advisor in India:

1. **Registration:** Apply for an insurance agent role through the website of the insurance company you would like to work with. Alternatively, you can register online via the IRDAI's portal.
2. **Training:** Complete the IRDA-mandated 15-hour foundational training program on insurance. This program can be taken online or in person.
3. **Exam and License:** Pass the IRDAI pre-licensing exam. This is a computer-based test with 50 questions, and you need a minimum of 17 points to pass. After passing the exam,

you will be eligible to receive your IRDAI license to work as an insurance advisor.

Here are some additional points to keep in mind:

- You must be at least 18 years old and have passed the 10th standard or equivalent examination to be eligible.
- Some states in India may have additional licensing requirements.

For more information on the IRDAI certification process, you can visit the IRDAI website or contact the insurance company you're interested in working with.

The financial investment to become an IRDA certified advisor in India is minimal. Here's a breakdown:

- **Training Fees:** The IRDAI-mandated training program might have a fee associated with it. This fee can vary depending on the provider you choose but is generally quite affordable. Expect it to be in the range of a few hundred rupees.
- **Exam Fees:** There's a nominal fee for taking the IRDAI pre-licensing exam, again a few hundred rupees.

Beyond these minimal fees, there is typically no major investment required. Some insurance companies might provide study materials or additional training programs, but these are often optional.

Here are some additional costs to consider, which aren't mandatory but might be helpful:

- **Study Materials:** You can purchase study guides or online resources to help you prepare for the exam. These are not essential but can be beneficial.
- **Travel:** Depending on where you take the training or exam, there might be travel costs involved.

Overall, becoming an IRDA certified advisor is an accessible career path with minimal financial barriers to entry. The focus is on your knowledge and ability to pass the exam.

FOOD FOR THOUGHT

— ❀ —

" Secure your financial future today with insurance, so you can live worry-free tomorrow. "

Chapter 8 - Investment

What is Investment?

In simple terms, investment involves using capital in the present to increase an asset's value over time.

Investing is like growing a seed. You put in something small (the seed, which is your money) today and wait for it to grow into something bigger (a plant, which is your money with extra money earned on it) in the future.

The goal of investing is to make your money work for you. You use your money to buy things that can make you more money over time. There are different ways to invest, but some common ones include:

- **Stocks:** Owning a small piece of a company and hoping it does well so its stock price goes up.
- **Bonds:** Loaning your money to a company or government and getting paid interest in return.
- **Savings accounts:** Putting your money in a bank and earning a small bit of interest.

There's always a chance that your investment won't grow or might even lose value. That's called risk. But generally, the longer you invest, the less risky it is.

Compounding

Compound interest is like earning interest on your interest, just like growing coriander seeds! You plant a few seeds (your principal amount), they sprout (you earn interest), and then those new coriander plants (your interest) also produce seeds (even more interest) in the next season.

Here's how it works:
- Imagine you invest ₹10,000 in a Fixed Deposit (FD) with a 5% annual interest rate.
- After one year, you'll earn ₹500 interest, bringing your total to ₹10,500.
- Now, the exciting part! In the second year, you don't just earn interest on the original ₹10,000. You also earn interest on the ₹500 you made earlier!
- So, in year two, you would earn a little more interest, around ₹525 (5% of ₹10,500).

This might seem like a small difference, but over time, like those coriander seeds multiplying, it can grow your money significantly. The longer you invest and the more frequently the interest is compounded (like multiple coriander harvests in a year), the faster your money grows.

This is why starting to save and invest early is important. It's like planting those coriander seeds - the sooner you start, the more harvests (interest) you'll get in the future!

10 Lakhs vs 1 Paisa - A Surprising Choice

One day, my mentor posed a seemingly straightforward yet thought-provoking question: Would you prefer an immediate lump sum of 10 lakhs INR or start with a single paisa that doubles in value every day for a month?

My instinctive response was to choose the 10 lakhs.

However, my mentor urged me to consider the alternative. He explained that by taking the doubling paisa, patience would be my guide. Initially, it seemed insignificant—just one paisa—but by the 28th day, it would exceed 13 lakhs, and by the 31st day, it would surpass 1 crore. This exemplified the power of exponential growth.

The 10 lakhs, while tempting, had limited growth potential. In contrast, the paisa highlighted the magic of compounding. My mentor drew parallels to investments, emphasizing the value of long-term thinking. For instance, a monthly investment of 25,000 INR at a 12% return rate could yield 40 lakhs in 8 years, 1 crore in 15 years, and a staggering 13 crores in 35 years.

Ultimately, the tale of the paisa and the 10 lakhs became a legend, teaching us that patience and strategic foresight lead to true prosperity.

Part 1 - Stock Market

In simple terms, the Stock market is a place where equity shares of companies are bought and sold by participants—both investors and traders.

Here's a brief overview:
1. Investors: They have a long-term horizon and benefit from capital appreciation over time. Their focus is on holding stocks for extended periods.

2. Traders: They seek quick profits by capitalizing on small price changes in equity shares, often within minutes or a single trading session.

In India, the Bombay Stock Exchange (BSE) and the National Stock Exchange (NSE) are major platforms for stock trading. Buyers and sellers place orders through brokers who offer online trading services. The settlement cycle follows a T+1 format, meaning trades are completed within one day. Understanding stock market terminology is essential for successful investing. Some common terms include bull market (rising market) and bear market (prolonged price declines).

Here's a quick breakdown:

- **Companies sell shares to get money**
- **People buy shares hoping they'll increase in value**
- **Stock exchanges like BSE and NSE manage the buying and selling**

It's important to remember that the stock market can be risky, and share prices can go up and down. But for those willing to take on that risk, it can be a way to grow their wealth over time.

Primary vs Secondary Market

The stock market you heard about is actually part of a larger system called the capital market, which has two main parts: the primary market and the secondary market.

- **Primary Market:** Think of this as the **birthplace** of new shares. This is where companies first issue and sell their shares to the public for the very first time. This is often done through an Initial Public Offering (IPO), which is basically a big announcement saying "We're a company going public, and you can now own a part of us!"
- **Secondary Market:** This is the familiar stock market you heard about earlier. Here, investors buy and sell shares **among themselves**. These are the shares that were already issued in the primary market. So, imagine it as a giant marketplace where people trade these existing shares like baseball cards, hoping to buy low and sell high. Examples of secondary markets in India are the Bombay Stock Exchange (BSE) and the National Stock Exchange (NSE).

Here's an analogy:

- **Primary Market:** Like a bakery selling fresh bread for the first time.

- **Secondary Market:** Like people buying and selling that bread amongst themselves after it leaves the bakery.

Both parts are important for the Indian financial system. The primary market helps companies raise capital, and the secondary market provides liquidity (the ease of buying and selling) for investors.

What is demat account and why do we need that?

Imagine you own a collection of rare trading cards. You wouldn't just keep them loose in your pocket, right? They could get lost or damaged easily.

That's where a demat account comes in. It's like a safe deposit box specifically for your shares and other financial securities in India. Instead of physical certificates, these holdings are stored electronically in a demat account. This offers several advantages:

- **Safety:** Shares are stored electronically, reducing the risk of loss or theft compared to physical certificates.
- **Convenience:** You can easily buy, sell, and hold shares all in one place. No more managing piles of paperwork!
- **Transparency:** You get clear records of your holdings and transactions. With a demat

account, you can easily track your investments and see how they're performing.

So, a demat account is essential for anyone who wants to participate in the Indian stock market securely and conveniently. In fact, it's mandatory to have one if you want to trade shares in India.

What is the role of stock brokers in stock market?

Stockbrokers act as intermediaries between investors and the stock market. Here's a breakdown of their key roles:

- **Execution of Trades:** They receive buy and sell orders from clients and execute them on the stock exchange. This ensures investors can participate in the market without directly interacting with the exchange.
- **Market Knowledge and Advice:** Traditionally, stockbrokers offered investment advice and guidance based on their understanding of the market and financial instruments. However, the extent of this service can vary depending on the type of broker.

- **Account Management:** Brokers often help with opening accounts, including demat accounts for holding securities, and managing them.
- **Regulatory Compliance:** Stockbrokers are subject to regulations to ensure fair and transparent practices in the market.

The role of stockbrokers has evolved with the rise of online trading platforms. Today, discount brokers offer commission-free trades, focusing just on order execution. However, full-service brokers may still provide in-depth advice and portfolio management services for a fee.

Different charges involved in stock market

There are several charges you'll encounter when trading stocks in India, broadly categorized into brokerage fees, exchange and regulatory charges, and government taxes. Here's a breakdown:

- **Brokerage Fees:** This is the fee charged by your stockbroker for executing your buy and sell orders. It can be a fixed amount per trade, a percentage of the trade value, or a combination of both. Some brokers offer zero brokerage plans for certain types of trades.

- **Exchange and Regulatory Charges:**
  - o **Transaction Charges:** These are levied by the stock exchange (NSE or BSE) on both buying and selling. The charges are a small percentage of the trade value.
  - o **SEBI Fees:** The Securities and Exchange Board of India (SEBI) charges a turnover fee on all transactions. This fee is a very small percentage of the trade value.
- **Government Taxes:**
  - o **Stamp Duty:** This is a state government levy on the value of shares purchased. The rate varies depending on the state.
  - o **GST (Goods and Services Tax):** This is a central tax levied on brokerage charges, transaction charges, and SEBI fees. The current GST rate is 18% (9% CGST + 9% SGST).

Additional Charges:

Demat Account Charges: Depository participants (DPs) charge fees for account maintenance and certain transactions like transferring securities.

- **Other Charges:** Brokers may levy other charges like account inactivity fees, margin interest (if you trade on margin), and fees for additional services like research reports or SMS alerts.

Remember: It's important to compare the charges levied by different brokers before opening an account. You can find detailed information on their websites or by contacting them directly.

Different instruments available in Indian stock market

The Indian stock market offers a variety of instruments for investors to participate in the capital market. Here are the main categories:

Equity (Shares):

- Represents ownership in a company. By buying shares, you become a part-owner of the company and are entitled to a portion of its profits (dividends).

- Equity is the most common instrument traded in the Indian stock market. There are two main types of equity shares:
    - **Common Shares:** Grant voting rights to shareholders and allow them to participate in company decisions.
    - **Preference Shares:** Offer a fixed dividend payout but do not have voting rights.

Debt Instruments:

- Represent a loan to a company or government. When you invest in debt instruments, you are essentially lending money to the issuer in exchange for fixed interest payments.
- Debt instruments are generally considered less risky than equities, as they offer a fixed return on your investment. However, the potential for capital appreciation is also lower. Some common types of debt instruments in India include:
    - **Bonds:** Issued by companies and governments to raise long-term capital.

- o **Debentures:** Unsecured debt instruments issued by companies.
- o **Government Bonds:** Issued by the Indian government to raise funds for various purposes.

Derivatives:

- Are contracts that derive their value from an underlying asset, such as a stock, commodity, or currency. Derivatives are used for various purposes, including hedging, speculation, and arbitrage.
- Derivatives are complex instruments and carry a high degree of risk. They are generally not suitable for beginner investors. Some common types of derivatives traded in India include:
  - o **Futures Contracts:** Agreements to buy or sell an asset at a predetermined price on a specific future date.
  - o **Options Contracts:** Contracts that give the buyer the right, but not the obligation, to buy or sell an underlying asset at a certain price by a certain date.

Other Instruments:

- **Mutual Funds:** Are pooled investment vehicles that invest in a basket of securities such as stocks, bonds, and other assets. Mutual funds are a good option for investors who want to diversify their portfolio and do not have the time or expertise to manage their own investments.
- **Exchange-Traded Funds (ETFs):** Are similar to mutual funds but are traded on stock exchanges like stocks. ETFs track a particular index or sector and offer a way to invest in a basket of securities with a single purchase.

The choice of instrument will depend on your investment goals, risk tolerance, and investment horizon. It's important to do your research and understand the risks involved before investing in any financial instrument.

Capital Gains Explained

A capital gain refers to the profit you make when you sell a capital asset for more than you originally paid for it. Capital assets can include a variety of things, such as:

- **Investments:** Stocks, bonds, mutual funds, real estate
- **Personal possessions:** Cars, boats, collectibles (depending on how long you've owned them)

There are two main factors that affect capital gains:

1. **Holding period:** How long you've owned the asset. This can impact the tax rate you pay on the capital gain.
2. **Sale price vs. purchase price:** The difference between what you sold the asset for and what you originally paid for it.

Calculating Capital Gains

The basic formula for calculating capital gains is:

Capital gain = Selling price - (Purchase price + Cost basis)

- **Selling price:** The amount you received when you sold the asset.
- **Purchase price:** The amount you originally paid for the asset.
- **Cost basis:** This can include any additional costs associated with acquiring the asset, such as commissions, fees, or improvements.

Here's a breakdown of how capital gains might be calculated for different instruments:

- **Stocks and Bonds:** In this case, the purchase price would be the original price you paid for the security, and the selling price would be the price you received when you sold it. Any commissions or fees paid would be factored into the cost basis.
- **Real Estate:** For real estate, the purchase price would include the original price you paid for the property, as well as any closing costs or realtor fees. The selling price would be the sale price of the property, minus any selling agent fees. Improvements made to the property may also be added to the cost basis.

Let's discuss the capital gains tax rates applicable there for stocks, bonds, mutual funds, and real estate:

Capital gains tax in India is categorized into two types:

- **Short-Term Capital Gains (STCG):** Applies to assets held for less than a specific holding period.

- **Long-Term Capital Gains (LTCG):** Applies to assets held for more than the specific holding period.

Here's a breakdown of current LTCG and STCG tax rates for the instruments you mentioned:

- **Stocks (Equity Shares):**
  - **LTCG:** 12.5% on gains exceeding Rs. 1.25 lakh in a financial year. This benefit of a lower tax rate applies to listed domestic equity shares held for over 12 months.
  - **STCG:** 20% for listed domestic equity shares held for less than 12 months.
- **Bonds:**
  - **LTCG:** Depends on the type of bond.
    - Debt mutual funds (considered bonds for taxation purposes): 20% with indexation benefit if held for over 3 years.
    - Listed bonds: Taxed at the investor's income tax slab rate if held for less than 3 years.
  - **STCG:** Not applicable for debt instruments held for less than 3

years, as they are taxed according to your income tax slab rate.

- **Mutual Funds:**
    - **Equity Mutual Funds:** Follow the same rules as stocks (mentioned above).
    - **Debt Mutual Funds:** Follow the same rules as bonds (mentioned above).
- **Real Estate:**
    - **LTCG:** 20% with indexation benefit if held for over 24 months. There can be exemptions if you reinvest the gains in specific ways.
    - **STCG:** Not applicable for real estate.

Important Note:

- These are the current tax rates as of June, 2024. Tax laws can change, so it's advisable to consult with a tax advisor for the most up-to-date information on capital gains tax in India.
- Additional factors like cess and surcharge may apply to the capital gains tax you pay.

Remember, this information is for general knowledge only and shouldn't be considered tax advice. Always consult with a qualified tax professional for personalized guidance on your specific situation.

Value Investing vs. Momentum Investing

These two strategies take opposite approaches to finding winning investments:

Value Investing

- **Focus:** Looks for undervalued stocks trading for less than their intrinsic value.
- **Analogy:** Like a bargain shopper, seeking stocks on sale.
- **Process:** Involves fundamental analysis of financial statements to assess a company's true worth. Looks for metrics like price-to-earnings (P/E) ratio, price-to-book (P/B) ratio, and dividend yield.
- **Patience:** Value investors are long-term players, willing to hold stocks for years until the market recognizes their true value.
- **Famous Practitioners:** Warren Buffett, Benjamin Graham.

Momentum Investing

- **Focus:** Chases stocks with upward price momentum, betting the trend will continue.

- **Analogy:** Riding a hot wave, buying stocks on a tear.
- **Process:** Utilizes technical analysis of charts and historical price movements to identify stocks with strong momentum.
- **Timing:** Momentum investors are short-term focused, aiming to capture quick gains as prices rise.
- **Risks:** More susceptible to market volatility and corrections, as trends can reverse quickly.

Here's a table summarizing the key differences:

Feature	Value Investing	Momentum Investing
Focus	Undervalued stocks	Stocks with upward price momentum
Analogy	Bargain shopping	Riding a hot wave
Process	Fundamental analysis	Technical analysis
Timeframe	Long-term (years)	Short-term (days, weeks)

Risks	Market may not recognize value quickly	Trend reversals and corrections
Famous Practitioners	Warren Buffett, Benjamin Graham	N/A

Choosing a Strategy:

- **Risk Tolerance:** Value investing is generally considered less risky due to its long-term approach.
- **Investment Horizon:** Value investing is better suited for long-term goals, while momentum investing can target short-term gains.
- **Research Skills:** Value investing requires in-depth financial analysis, while momentum investing relies on technical analysis.

Remember, diversification is key! You can incorporate elements of both strategies or choose one that best suits your goals and risk tolerance.

Portfolio Analysis

Regular portfolio analysis, review, and rebalancing are crucial for staying on track with your investment goals. Here's why:

- **Maintain Risk-Return Balance:** Markets fluctuate, causing your asset allocation (mix of stocks, bonds, etc.) to drift from your target. This can increase risk if you become overexposed to volatile assets or decrease returns if you become too conservative. Rebalancing brings it back to your desired level.
- **Identify Opportunities & Risks:** Regular analysis helps you spot underperforming assets that might need replacing or strong performers you might want to take profits from. It also helps identify potential risks you weren't aware of, like an entire sector struggling.
- **Stay Aligned with Goals:** Your life and financial goals might change over time. Reviewing your portfolio ensures it's still aligned with your needs. Maybe you need to adjust for retirement or a growing family.

Effort and Time Involved:

The effort and time involved can vary depending on your portfolio complexity and how you choose to do it. Here's a breakdown:

- **Simple Analysis & Review:** You can do a basic analysis using online tools or financial apps. This might involve checking asset allocation percentages and basic performance metrics. Time commitment: Minimal (think 15-30 minutes quarterly).

- **In-Depth Analysis:** This involves delving deeper into individual holdings, researching market trends, and potentially using professional software. Time commitment: More involved (several hours per quarter).
- **Rebalancing:** This can involve buying or selling assets to get back to your target allocation. You can do it manually through your brokerage platform or set up automatic rebalancing features (if offered). Time commitment: Varies depending on the extent of rebalancing needed.

Tips for Efficiency:

- **Set a Schedule:** Decide on a frequency for analysis and review (quarterly or annually).
- **Automate What You Can:** Use online tools and portfolio trackers for basic analysis.
- **Seek Professional Help:** For complex portfolios or if you're uncomfortable, consider consulting a financial advisor.

Remember, even a basic level of analysis and review is better than none. By dedicating some time regularly, you can ensure your portfolio stays on track to meet your long-term goals.

Analysis Tools

Technical Analysis Tools

Technical analysts use a variety of tools to analyze historical price and volume data to identify trading opportunities. Some of the most common technical analysis tools include:

- **Charts:** Charts are the foundation of technical analysis. They allow you to visualize price movements over time and identify trends, support and resistance levels, and other technical indicators.
- **Indicators:** Technical indicators are mathematical calculations that are used to identify trends, generate buy and sell signals, and measure volatility. Some of the most popular technical indicators include moving averages, relative strength index (RSI), and Bollinger Bands.
- **Drawing tools:** Drawing tools are used to identify trends, support and resistance levels, and chart patterns. Some of the most common drawing tools include trendlines, channels, and Fibonacci retracements.

TradingView: Supercharged Charting and Social Network

TradingView is a popular platform that combines several features for traders and investors:

- **Interactive Charts:** It offers advanced charting tools for in-depth technical analysis of various financial instruments like stocks, forex, futures, and even cryptocurrencies. You can utilize technical indicators, drawing tools, and a wide range of chart types to identify trends and make trading decisions.
- **Social Network:** TradingView goes beyond just charting. It functions as a social network for traders where you can:
    - Share your analysis and trading ideas with others.
    - Discuss market trends and strategies with other users.
    - Follow successful traders and potentially learn from their approaches.
- **Mobile App:** TradingView offers a mobile app so you can access your charts, analysis, and the social network features on the go.
- **Free and Paid Plans:** There's a free plan with basic features, while paid subscriptions unlock additional functionalities like real-time data, advanced charting tools, and increased customization options.

Fundamental Analysis Tools

Fundamental analysts use a variety of tools to analyze a company's financial statements and other relevant data to assess its intrinsic value. Some of the most common fundamental analysis tools include:

- **Financial statements:** Financial statements are a company's financial reports that provide information about its financial performance and position. The three main financial statements are the income statement, the balance sheet, and the cash flow statement.
- **Financial ratios:** Financial ratios are used to assess a company's profitability, solvency, liquidity, and efficiency. Some of the most common financial ratios include the price-to-earnings (P/E) ratio, the debt-to-equity ratio, and the return on equity (ROE).
- **Industry analysis:** Industry analysis involves researching the economic conditions, competitive landscape, and regulatory environment of a particular industry.
- **Company analysis:** Company analysis involves researching a company's management team, business model, competitive advantages, and future growth prospects.

Screener Platforms: Finding Potential Investments
Screener platforms are another valuable tool for investors. They help you identify potential investment opportunities by filtering a large universe of stocks based on various criteria. Some

features you might find on screener platforms include:

- **Fundamental Analysis Filters:** You can screen stocks based on financial ratios like P/E ratio, debt-to-equity ratio, or return on equity. This helps you find companies with strong financial performance.
- **Technical Analysis Filters:** Some screeners allow filtering based on technical indicators like moving averages or RSI. This can help you identify stocks that are trending or oversold/overbought.
- **Industry and Sector Focus:** You can focus on specific industries or sectors that interest you.
- **Additional Criteria:** Screeners may allow filtering by factors like market capitalization, dividend yield, or recent news sentiment.

Key Differences:

TradingView is primarily focused on technical analysis through its advanced charting tools and social features. While it may offer some fundamental analysis, screeners excel at filtering stocks based on various fundamental and technical criteria to help you discover potential investments.

Choosing the Right Tool:

Both TradingView and screener platforms can be valuable tools for investors depending on your needs.

- If you're a technical analyst who actively trades and wants advanced charting and social interaction, TradingView might be a good fit.
- If you're an investor looking to identify potential investments based on fundamental and technical factors, a screener platform could be more helpful.

Consider your investment style and goals when deciding which tool (or potentially both) would be most beneficial for you.

Part 2 - Mutual funds

Imagine a pizza party. Instead of buying a whole pizza yourself, you chip in money with your friends to buy a bigger pizza. That way, everyone gets a slice and you can try different toppings!

A mutual fund is kind of like that pizza party for investing. It's a pool of money from many people that's used to buy various investments, like stocks and bonds. A professional manager oversees the fund, like choosing the pizza toppings. This way, you get a slice (share) of a diversified investment portfolio, without having to pick all the investments yourself.

Mutual funds are generally less risky than buying individual stocks because your money is spread across different investments. And hopefully, like a delicious pizza, your investment will grow over time!

Types of Mutual Funds

There are many different types of mutual funds available in India, each with its own investment objective and risk profile. Here's a breakdown of the two main ways mutual funds is categorized:

By Investment Objective

- **Equity Funds:** These funds invest primarily in stocks of companies. They offer the potential for high returns but also carry higher risk.
- **Debt Funds:** These funds invest in fixed-income securities like bonds and

government securities. They offer lower risk and predictable returns compared to equity funds.

- **Hybrid Funds:** These funds invest in a mix of equity and debt instruments, offering a balance between risk and return.
- **Liquid Funds:** These funds invest in short-term debt instruments like commercial paper and treasury bills. They offer high liquidity and low risk, making them suitable for parking your emergency fund.

Fund of Funds

Imagine you want to order a bunch of different dishes from various restaurants, but don't have the time or expertise to pick the best ones from each place. A food delivery app that curates' meals from different restaurants might be helpful, right?

A fund of funds works similarly in the investment world. Instead of directly buying stocks or bonds, it invests your money in a basket of other mutual funds. This offers several benefits:

- **Diversification:** By spreading your money across multiple funds, you reduce risk. Even if one fund performs poorly, others might make up for it.

- **Professional Management:** The fund manager of the fund of funds picks and chooses the underlying mutual funds, saving you research time. Ideally, they select funds with strong performance and complementary investment styles.
- **Access to Expertise:** Fund of funds might invest in niche funds or those requiring a high minimum investment, which might be out of reach for individual investors.

However, there are also some downsides to consider:

- **Fees:** Since you're paying fees for both the fund of funds and the underlying funds, the overall expense ratio might be higher.
- **Less Control:** You have less control over the specific investments within the fund of funds compared to choosing individual mutual funds.

Global Funds

A global fund is a type of mutual fund that invests in companies located around the world, not just in your home country. This allows you to:

- **Diversify Geographically:** By spreading your investments across different countries, you can reduce the impact of economic downturns in any single region.

- **Tap into Growing Markets:** Global funds can give you exposure to fast-growing economies in other parts of the world.
- **Benefit from Currency Fluctuations:** If the value of the foreign currency your global fund invests in goes up, it can boost your returns.

However, keep in mind that global funds can be more complex and potentially riskier than domestic funds due to factors like currency fluctuations and political instability in certain regions.

Feature	Fund of Funds	Global Funds
Invests in	Other mutual funds	Stocks and bonds of companies worldwide
Diversification	Across different mutual funds	Across different countries
Management	By the fund of funds manager	By the fund manager

Potential Benefits	Reduced risk, access to expertise	Geographic diversification, exposure to growing markets
Potential Drawbacks	Higher fees, less control	More complex, currency risk, political risk

By Structure

- **Open-Ended Funds:** These are the most common types of mutual funds. You can buy and redeem units of these funds at any time during trading hours.
- **Close-Ended Funds:** These funds have a fixed maturity period. You can only buy and sell units on stock exchanges like shares.
- **Interval Funds:** These are a mix of open-ended and closed-ended funds. They offer periodic windows for investors to redeem their units.

Choosing the right type of mutual fund for you depends on your investment goals, risk tolerance, and investment horizon. It's always best to consult with a financial advisor before making any investment decisions.

Different channels to buy mutual funds in India
In India, you have a few options to choose from when it comes to buying mutual funds, each with its own set of pros and cons:

Direct Channel:
- Invest directly with the mutual fund company on their website or mobile app.
- Lower expense ratio (fees) since there's no intermediary involved.
- Requires you to do your own research and manage your investments.

Advisor Channel:
- Seek guidance from a registered financial advisor who can recommend funds based on your goals and risk tolerance.
- Advisors can provide personalized advice and hand-holding throughout the investment process.
- Typically comes with a fee for the advisor's services.

Regular Plan (Distributor Channel):
- Purchase mutual funds through distributors like banks, NBFCs (Non-Banking Financial Companies), or independent financial advisors.
- Distributors might offer convenience and wider access to various funds.
- May involve higher expense ratios compared to the direct channel.

Online Platforms:
- Invest through online platforms offered by discount brokers or fintech startups.
- Often provide a user-friendly interface for buying and managing your investments. Fees can vary depending on the platform.

Stock Exchanges (NSE MFSS & BSE StAR MF):
- Purchase and sell mutual fund units on stock exchanges like you would trade stocks.
- Requires a demat account and trading experience.
- Less common for beginners due to the stock exchange environment.

MF Utility (MFU):
- A convenient platform for online transactions across participating mutual funds.
- Allows consolidated account statements and facilitates easy switching between funds.
- Requires registration with MFU and your chosen fund houses.

Considering factors like your investment experience, comfort level with research, and desired level of guidance will help you choose the most suitable channel for buying mutual funds in India.

Different investment strategies to buy with mutual funds

SIP, lumpsum, STP, and SWP are all investment strategies used with mutual funds, but they serve different purposes:

SIP (Systematic Investment Plan):
- Think of it as a **regular savings plan** for mutual funds. You invest a **fixed amount** at **predefined intervals** (weekly, monthly, quarterly) over a long period.
- **Benefits:**
    - **Rupee-cost averaging:** You buy units at different price points, potentially averaging out the cost per unit over time.
    - **Discipline:** Encourages regular investment and builds financial discipline.
    - **Suitable for:** Long-term goals, beginners, those with limited capital.

Lumpsum Investment:
- This is a **one-time, large investment** in a mutual fund scheme.
- **Benefits:**
    - Potentially takes advantage of a lower entry point in the market.
    - Simpler to manage compared to SIP.

  - **Suitable for:** Investors with a substantial amount available, those targeting a specific investment goal.

STP (Systematic Transfer Plan):
- This involves the **systematic transfer of a fixed amount** from one mutual fund scheme (source scheme) to another (target scheme) at regular intervals.
- **Benefits:**
  - Allows you to gradually shift your investment from debt to equity (common strategy) as your risk tolerance evolves.
  - Maintains liquidity in the source scheme while investing in the target scheme.
  - **Suitable for:** Asset allocation strategy, risk management.

SWP (Systematic Withdrawal Plan):
- This allows you to **withdraw a fixed amount** from your mutual fund scheme at regular intervals. You redeem units to get the money.
- **Benefits:**
  - Provides a **regular income stream** from your investments.
  - Useful for retirees or those needing periodic payouts.

- o **Suitable for:** Generating income from your investments, retirement planning.

Choosing the right approach depends on your financial goals, risk tolerance, and investment horizon. Consider consulting a financial advisor for personalized guidance.

Power of compounding

Mutual funds and the power of compounding are a perfect match for growing your wealth over time.

Here's how they work together:
- **Mutual Funds Pool Your Money:** When you invest in a mutual fund, you're essentially putting your money together with other investors. This allows you to invest in a diversified portfolio of stocks or bonds, even with a smaller amount of money.
- **Compounding Grows Your Returns:** The power of compounding refers to earning returns on your returns. In a mutual fund, any dividends or capital gains earned by the fund are typically reinvested back into the fund. This means your returns are compounded, growing your total investment over time.

Let's see an example:

Imagine you invest Rs. 10,000 in a mutual fund that earns a 10% annual return. Here's how compounding works:

- **Year 1:** You earn Rs. 1,000 (10% of Rs. 10,000) in returns. The fund reinvests this, so your total investment becomes Rs. 11,000 (Rs. 10,000 original + Rs. 1,000 return).
- **Year 2:** You earn another 10% return, but this time it's calculated at Rs. 11,000, which is Rs. 1,100. So your total investment grows to Rs. 12,100 (Rs. 11,000 + Rs. 1,100).

As you can see, even with a constant return rate, the amount of money you earn increases each year due to compounding.

Benefits of Compounding with Mutual Funds:

- **Start Early:** The longer your investment horizon (the time you stay invested), the greater the benefit of compounding. Starting to invest early in your life allows your money to grow exponentially over time.
- **Regular Investments:** Regular investments through SIP (Systematic Investment Plan) in mutual funds add to the compounding effect. Even small amounts invested consistently can lead to significant growth over the long term.
- **Professional Management:** Mutual funds are managed by professionals who actively

manage the portfolio, potentially leading to higher returns that can be compounded.

Remember: While mutual funds offer the potential for compounded growth, they also involve market risks. Investments can go down in value, and you may not get back your original investment. It's important to choose funds that align with your risk tolerance and investment goals.

How to become a registered Mutual Funds Distributor (MFD)

NISM Series V-A Mutual Fund Distributors Certification Examination is a mandatory requirement to become a registered Mutual Funds Distributor (MFD) in India. Here's how to get it:

1. **Eligibility:** You must be 18 years or above and have completed a minimum of three years of bachelor's degree from a recognized educational institution.

2. **Enroll for the NISM-Series-V-A Exam:** The National Institute of Securities Markets (NISM) conducts the exam. You can register online on the NISM website https://certifications.nism.ac.in/.

3. **Prepare for the Exam:** NISM offers study material and sample papers on their website. You can also find various coaching

institutes and online resources to help you prepare.

4. **Take the Exam:** The exam is computer-based and consists of 100 multiple-choice questions. You need to score at least 50% to pass.

5. **Obtain ARN (AMFI Registration Number):** After passing the exam, you need to apply for an ARN from the Association of Mutual Funds in India (AMFI). This allows you to associate with mutual fund companies and sell their products.

Additional Points:

- The NISM Series V-A certificate has a validity period of three years. You need to complete Continuing Professional Education (CPE) programs to renew it.
- You can directly approach mutual fund companies or join online platforms like Nivesh to start distributing their funds after obtaining your ARN.

Part 3 - Gold

There are a few reasons why gold holds such a special place in India:

- **Cultural Significance:** For centuries, gold has been woven into the fabric of Indian culture.

It's seen as auspicious and plays a role in festivals, religious ceremonies, and especially weddings. Gold jewelry is often passed down as heirlooms, strengthening family ties.

- **Financial Security:** In a country where access to formal banking might be limited, particularly in rural areas, gold is a trusted way to store wealth. It's seen as a safe-haven, especially during economic uncertainty. Since it holds its value well, people can sell their gold for cash if needed.
- **Symbol of Status:** Gold jewelry is a sign of prosperity and social standing. Owning gold demonstrates achievement and brings respect. This is especially true for weddings, where elaborate gold jewelry is a significant part of the bride's attire.

Now, about the price of gold:
- **Global Market:** Gold is a global commodity, and its price is set on international markets. Factors like inflation, interest rates, and global economic conditions all influence the price.
- **High Demand:** India is the world's largest gold consumer, and its strong demand plays a role in influencing the global price.
- **Limited Supply:** Gold is a finite resource, and there's only so much of it available. This,

combined with high demand, can drive prices up.

It's important to note that gold prices do fluctuate, and while they generally trend upwards, there can be dips.

Physical vs Virtual Gold

Both physical and virtual gold have their own advantages and disadvantages, making the best choice depend on your investment goals. Here's a breakdown to help you decide:

Physical Gold:
Pros:

- **Tangible Asset:** You actually hold the gold, offering a sense of security and control.
- **Cultural Significance:** Important for some cultures and traditional uses like jewelry.
- **Potential Liquidity:** You can sell it to pawn shops or jewelers, though melt value might be lower.

Cons:

- **Storage Costs:** You need a safe deposit box or secure storage, which adds an expense.
- **Security Risk:** Theft or loss is a concern.
- **Transaction Costs:** Selling physical gold often involves fees and takes time.

- **Making Charges:** When buying jewelry, a portion of the cost goes towards crafting, not the gold itself.

Virtual Gold:
Pros:
- **Convenience:** Easy to buy and sell online in small amounts.
- **Lower Costs:** No storage fees or making charges.
- **Security:** Usually stored by the provider in insured vaults.
- **Liquidity:** Often easier to sell quickly on online platforms.

Cons:
- **Not Tangible:** You don't physically hold the gold, which some find less secure.
- **Limited Uses:** Can't be used for jewelry or cultural traditions.
- **Counterparty Risk:** Relies on the provider to actually hold the gold they represent.
- **Tax Implications:** Tax treatment for virtual gold can vary depending on the type (e.g., SGB vs. ETF).

Here are some additional factors to consider:
- **Investment Horizon:** For long-term holding, physical gold might be suitable. For shorter-term trading, virtual might be easier.

- **Risk Tolerance:** If security is a major concern, physical gold might be better. If convenience is important, virtual might be preferable.

Ultimately, the best choice depends on your individual needs and preferences. Do some research to understand the different types of virtual gold (SGBs, ETFs) and their specifics before investing.

SGB and its benefits

SGB stands for Sovereign Gold Bond. It's a government-backed way to invest in gold without actually holding the physical metal. Here's the breakdown:

What is an SGB?

- Issued by the Reserve Bank of India (RBI) on behalf of the Indian government.
- Essentially a certificate representing a specific amount of gold (in grams).
- Functions like a bond, with a fixed maturity period (typically 8 years).

Benefits of SGBs:

- **Safe and Secure:** Backed by the government, reducing default risk.
- **Convenient:** No need for secure storage or worrying about theft.
- **Earns Interest:** SGBs pay a fixed annual interest rate in addition to the gold price movement.

- **Tax Advantages:** Redemption at maturity is tax-free (capital gains tax). There are also benefits on interest earned (check with a tax advisor for specifics).
- **Liquidity:** SGBs can be traded on the secondary market after the lock-in period (usually 5 years).

Note - New SGB bonds are not issued right now by the Government, but the old issues are traded in the stock Exchanges.

Here's a quick comparison of Physical vs. SGB Gold:

Feature	Physical Gold	SGB
Form	Tangible metal	Certificate
Storage	Requires safekeeping	Stored by RBI or in Demat form
Security Risk	Theft or loss possible	Lower risk, government backed
Liquidity	Selling can be slow	Can be traded after lock-in period

Making Charges	Price includes crafting cost	No extra charges
Interest	No interest	Pays fixed annual interest
Taxes	May incur capital gains tax	Maturity redemption tax-free (capital gains)

Remember: SGBs track the price of gold, so their value goes up and down along with the gold market. They are a good option for those who want to invest in gold but avoid the hassles of physical ownership. However, they do have a lock-in period and may not be suitable for everyone.

Gold and Silver mutual funds

Gold and silver mutual funds are a type of mutual fund that invests in gold and silver, either directly or indirectly. Here's a breakdown of how they work:

Types of Gold and Silver Mutual Funds:
- **Gold ETFs (Exchange Traded Funds):** These funds invest in gold Bullion (physical gold) stored in secure vaults. The price of the mutual fund unit reflects the price of the underlying gold.

- **Silver ETFs:** Similar to gold ETFs, but invest in silver bullion.
- **Gold and Silver FoFs (Fund of Funds):** These funds invest in other gold or silver ETFs, providing diversification within the precious metals space.

Benefits of Gold and Silver Mutual Funds:
- **Convenience:** No need to store physical gold or silver, which eliminates storage costs and security risks.
- **Lower Investment:** You can invest in smaller amounts compared to buying physical gold or silver.
- **Professional Management:** Experienced fund managers handle the investment decisions.
- **Liquidity:** You can easily buy and sell units on the stock exchange (for ETFs).
- **Diversification:** Gold and silver can add diversification to your portfolio, potentially reducing overall risk.

Things to Consider:
- **Expense Ratio:** Fees charged by the fund manager, which can impact your returns.
- **Price Fluctuations:** Gold and silver prices can be volatile, so the value of your investment can go up and down.

- **Not Direct Ownership:** You don't directly own the physical gold or silver, but rather units in the mutual fund.
- **Tax Implications:** Capital gains taxes may apply when you sell your units.

Are Gold and Silver Mutual Funds Right for You?
These funds can be a good option for investors who want exposure to gold and silver without the hassles of physical ownership. However, they are not suitable for everyone. Here are some things to consider:

- **Investment Goals:** Align with your overall investment strategy and risk tolerance.
- **Investment Horizon:** Gold and silver are often seen as long-term investments.

It's always wise to do your research and consult a financial advisor before investing in any mutual fund, including gold and silver ones.

FOOD FOR THOUGHT

" *Your money should be working harder than you do. Invest wisely in stocks and mutual funds for a financially secure future.* "

Chapter 9 - Retirement Planning

Retirement planning is basically setting yourself up for a financially secure future after you stop working. It involves figuring out how much money you'll need to cover your living expenses in retirement, and then creating a plan to save and invest that amount.

Here's why it's important?:

Maintain your standard of living: You probably want to keep enjoying your hobbies and maybe even travel after retirement. Planning ensures you have the money to do that.

Financial security: Retirement savings act as a safety net in case of unexpected expenses or medical bills.

Peace of mind: Knowing you've planned for your future reduces stress and lets you focus on enjoying your retirement.

Even if retirement seems far off, starting early gives your savings more time to grow through compound interest. The earlier you start, the smaller the amount you need to set aside each month.

Inflation

Inflation refers to the gradual increase in prices for goods and services over time. Think of it like the buying power of your money slowly decreasing. A loaf of bread that costs 50 INR today might cost 60 INR in a year due to inflation.

Here's why inflation is crucial in retirement planning:

- **Erosion of purchasing power:** Over time, inflation eats away at the value of your saved money. If you plan based on today's prices, you might underestimate how much you'll actually need in retirement years down the line.
- **Long-term planning:** Retirement can last 20-30 years or even longer. Factoring in inflation ensures your savings keep pace with rising costs of living throughout your retirement.

To account for inflation, you should estimate an inflation rate and factor that into your retirement calculations. This will help you determine a more realistic savings goal to maintain your desired lifestyle after retirement.

Cost of Living

The cost of living refers to the amount of money you need to maintain a certain standard of living in a particular place. It includes expenses like housing, food, transportation, healthcare, and utilities.

There's no single reason why the cost of living increases every year, but here are some major factors:

- **Inflation:** As mentioned earlier, inflation is the general rise in prices. This can be caused by factors like:
    - **Increased demand:** When demand for goods and services goes up, businesses can raise prices because people are willing to pay more.
    - **Supply chain disruptions:** If there are issues getting raw materials or finished products to market, prices can rise due to scarcity.
    - **Rising production costs:** If the cost of labor, materials, or energy increases, businesses may pass those costs on to consumers.
- **Housing costs:** Housing is a major expense for most people, and housing costs tend to rise over time due to limited space, increasing demand, and construction costs.
- **Healthcare costs:** Medical care and services tend to get more expensive year after year due to advancements in technology, rising drug costs, and an aging population.

It's important to note that the rate of increase in the cost of living can vary depending on location and individual circumstances. Some areas, like major cities, might see a faster rise in costs compared to rural areas.

By understanding the cost of living and how it changes, you can make informed financial decisions. This could involve budgeting, negotiating raises to keep pace with inflation, or considering ways to reduce expenses.

Concept of third child for Retirement

Want to secure your golden years? Consider a Systematic Investment Plan (SIP) – like spending for your third child to save for retirement. Here's how it works:

- **Invest regularly:** Start by investing ₹17,000 every month (2 Lakhs every year). Consistency is key!
- **Grow your nest egg:** Over 15 years, with a potential 12% annual growth rate (CAGR), your investment could reach a whopping ₹80 Lakhs!
- **Let it compound:** Leave that money invested for another 10 years to benefit from compound interest. Imagine it growing on its own! By the end of these 10 years, your investment could be worth ₹2.5 crore.

- **Create retirement income:** Set up a Systematic Withdrawal Plan (SWP) to withdraw a steady ₹1 Lakh monthly income throughout your retirement.
- **Beat inflation:** Increase your withdrawal amount by 10% each year to keep pace with inflation.

The result? Even after 20 years of withdrawals, you could potentially have a remaining corpus of ₹1.5 Crore!

Remember, the best time to start investing for your third child (retirement) is today!

Start investing today and build a secure and comfortable retirement for yourself!

FOOD FOR THOUGHT

" Retirement is a journey, not a destination. Plan wisely to ensure you have the resources to enjoy the view. "

Chapter 10 - Estate Planning

Estate planning is essentially making arrangements for how your stuff (stuff = assets and debts) will be handled after you die or become incapacitated. It's about ensuring your wishes are carried out smoothly and efficiently, minimizing stress and confusion for those you leave behind. Here's a breakdown of the key aspects:

1. Planning for Distribution:
- **Who gets what:** This involves specifying who inherits your belongings, money, property, etc. You'll name beneficiaries - the people or organizations receiving your assets.
- **How they receive it:** You can decide if they inherit everything at once, in stages, or under certain conditions.

2. Minimizing Taxes and Costs:
- Estate planning can help reduce the amount your estate pays in taxes and legal fees. This can be achieved through strategies like trusts and beneficiary designations on accounts.

3. Incapacity Planning:
- What happens if you can't make decisions for yourself? Estate planning allows you to appoint someone you trust (a power of

attorney) to manage your finances and healthcare if you become incapacitated.

4. Guardianship for Minor Children:
- If you have minor children, you can designate a guardian to care for them in the event of your death.

Common Estate Planning Tools:
- **Will:** A legal document outlining your wishes for asset distribution and guardianship of minor children.
- **Trust:** A legal entity that holds assets and distributes them according to your instructions, potentially avoiding probate (court process for distributing assets).
- **Power of Attorney:** Grants someone the legal authority to manage your finances and property if you're unable.
- **Advance Directive (Living Will):** Specifies your medical care preferences in case you can't communicate them.

Importance of Estate Planning:
- Ensures your wishes are respected.
- Reduces stress and confusion for loved ones during a difficult time.
- Minimizes taxes and legal fees.
- Provides peace of mind knowing your affairs are in order.

Who Needs Estate Planning?

Estate planning is often thought of for the wealthy, but it's beneficial for everyone. Even if you have modest assets, you'll still want to make sure your loved ones are taken care of and avoid unnecessary legal complications.

Real Life Examples: From Riches To Rags

The Tragic Tale Of Raymond Founder Vijaypat Singhania

Textile tycoon Vijaypat Singhania's life showcases the importance of estate planning. Despite achieving immense success, his strained relationship with his son has resulted in legal battles and uncertainty surrounding his business and personal affairs. This situation could have been avoided with clear communication and a legally binding will. Singhania's story serves as a cautionary tale, emphasizing the need to plan for the future and ensure your wishes are known to prevent family conflict and turmoil.

Aretha Franklin's Estate

The legendary singer Aretha Franklin passed away in 2018 without a will. This resulted in a lengthy legal battle between her four sons over her estate, which included royalties, recordings, and other assets. The situation caused unnecessary stress and division within the family, and it took years to reach a settlement.

These cases demonstrate the importance of having a will, especially for those with significant assets. A will allows you to clearly define who inherits your belongings and minimizes the chances of conflict among loved ones after you're gone.

Estate plan disputes can arise due to various situations

- **Sibling Rivalry and Competition**: Siblings may contest the distribution of assets.
- **Stepchild Disputes:** Complex blended families can lead to disagreements.
- **Second and Subsequent Marriage Claims:** Conflicts may arise between children from different marriages.
- **Estranged Family Inclusion:** Including estranged family members can cause tension.
- **Close Family Exclusion:** Omitting close family members can lead to disputes.
- **Resentment and Emotional Tension**: Unresolved emotions can fuel disagreements.

Effective strategies to minimize family disputes during estate planning

- **Clear Communication:** Regularly communicate your decisions and reasons to your family. Hold family meetings to allow everyone to express their thoughts and concerns. Document your wishes and share copies with beneficiaries to ensure understanding.

- **Choose the Right Executor:** Select an executor who remains neutral and fair, even if tensions arise. Look for someone with organizational skills and effective communication abilities. Consider a professional fiduciary (e.g., a bank or trust company) to manage your estate impartially.
- **Utilize Mediation:** A neutral third-party mediator can help resolve disputes. Mediation is less adversarial and more cost-effective than litigation.
- **Create a Detailed Estate Plan:** Include clear instructions on asset management and distribution. Cover components like wills, trusts, powers of attorney, and healthcare directives. Remember, thoughtful planning and open communication can significantly reduce the potential for family conflicts during estate planning.

Getting Started:

Consider consulting with an estate planning attorney to discuss your specific needs and create a plan that works for you. There are also online resources and tools available to help you get started with basic planning.

FOOD FOR THOUGHT

" Your legacy isn't just about what you build, but how it's passed on."

Chapter 11 - Stock Market Trading

Stock market trading refers to the buying and selling of shares (ownership pieces) of companies on a stock exchange. It's a way to invest in businesses and potentially profit from their growth. Here's a breakdown:

- **Buying and Selling Shares:** You buy shares hoping they'll increase in value, allowing you to sell them later for a profit.
- **Stock Exchanges:** These are marketplaces where stock trades happen. India has two main ones: the National Stock Exchange (NSE) and the Bombay Stock Exchange (BSE).
- **Price Fluctuations:** Stock prices constantly change based on supply, demand, and company performance.

Trading vs. Investing

Stock market trading can be short-term, aiming to capitalize on quick price movements. Long-term investing focuses on holding shares for years, hoping the company grows in value.

Trading Options in India

India offers various trading options to suit different goals and risk tolerances. Here are a few common ones:

- **Day Trading:** Buying and selling stocks within a single trading day.
- **Positional Trading:** Holding stocks for a few days, weeks, or months based on a particular strategy.
- **Swing Trading:** Holding stocks for short-term to mid-term trends, lasting from weeks to months.
- **Long-Term Investing:** Buying and holding stocks for years or even decades, aiming for long-term growth.

Options Trading

Options are derivative contracts that allow investors to speculate on the future price movement of an underlying asset (such as a stock or index) without owning the asset itself.

In India, the most commonly traded index options are the **Nifty 50** and the **Nifty Bank**. These options are based on the NSE's Nifty index and the banking sector index, respectively.

Key points about options trading:
Call Options: These give the holder the right (but not the obligation) to buy the underlying asset at a specified price (strike price) before a specific date (expiry).
Put Options: These give the holder the right (but not the obligation) to sell the underlying asset at a specified price (strike price) before expiry.

Liquidity: Options contracts should have sufficient liquidity for efficient trading.
Volatility: Options thrive in volatile markets, as price fluctuations create opportunities.
Strategies: Traders use various strategies, such as covered calls, protective puts, and spreads, to manage risk and enhance returns

Remember, stock market trading involves inherent risks. It's crucial to research, understand the different options, and choose a strategy that aligns with your financial goals and risk appetite.

Options Trading in India - A Suicide Mission?
Let's delve deeper into the psychological toll of options trading. As traders, we often focus on the financial aspects, but it's crucial to recognize the emotional impact. Here are some key points to consider:

1. **Stress and Anxiety:**
   - Options trading can be nerve-wracking. The constant monitoring of positions, market news, and price fluctuations can lead to heightened stress levels.
   - Anxiety arises from uncertainty—whether it's waiting for an option to expire or facing unexpected market movements.

2. **Loss Aversion:**
   - Humans are wired to feel losses more intensely than gains. When an options trade goes south, the emotional impact can be significant.
   - Fear of losing money can lead to irrational decisions, such as holding onto losing positions longer than necessary.

3. **Sleepless Nights:**
   - Traders often lose sleep over their positions. The fear of waking up to a substantial loss can be overwhelming.
   - Sleep deprivation affects decision-making and overall well-being.

4. **Overconfidence and Ego:**
   - A string of successful trades can inflate our ego. Overconfidence may lead to riskier bets.
   - When the market humbles us, the emotional blow can be severe.

5. **Isolation and Loneliness:**
   - Trading can be isolating. Hours spent analyzing charts and executing trades can distance us from social interactions.

- Loneliness exacerbates stress and affects mental health.

6. **Depression and Despair:**
   - Sustained losses can trigger feelings of depression. Financial setbacks impact self-worth and outlook on life.
   - Traders may feel trapped, unable to escape the cycle of losses.

7. **Seeking Validation and Coping Mechanisms:**
   - Traders seek validation from peers, forums, or social media. Positive feedback reinforces their choices.
   - Coping mechanisms include denial, blaming external factors, or doubling down on risky trades.

Conclusion: Options trading isn't just about numbers; it's about emotions too. Acknowledging the psychological toll is essential. As traders, we must prioritize mental well-being, seek support, and practice self-awareness. Approaching options trading with caution, a thorough understanding of the risks, and a well-defined strategy is vital for Indian investors. By equipping yourself with knowledge and adopting responsible trading practices, you can increase your chances of navigating the market effectively.

Automation (ALGO) Trading

Algo trading, also known as automated trading, is a method of using computer programs to execute trades in the Indian stock market. These programs are designed to analyze market data, identify trading opportunities based on your set criteria, and then automatically buy or sell securities according to your predefined instructions.

Here's a breakdown of algo trading in India:

Benefits:

- **Speed and Accuracy:** Algorithms can react to market changes much faster than humans, allowing you to capitalize on fleeting opportunities.
- **Emotionless Trading:** By removing emotions from the decision-making process, algos can execute trades based on logic and pre-set rules.
- **Back-testing:** You can test your trading strategies on historical data to see how they would have performed before deploying them with real capital.
- **24/7 Trading:** Algorithmic programs can monitor the market continuously, allowing you to trade around the clock.

Things to Consider:

- **Programming Knowledge:** While some platforms offer pre-built algos, creating your own often requires programming knowledge.
- **Costs:** Brokerage fees for algo trading can be higher than traditional trading.
- **Market Risks:** Algo trading doesn't guarantee profits, and unexpected market movements can still lead to losses.
- **Technical Issues:** Technical glitches or software malfunctions can disrupt your trading activity.

Getting Started with Algo Trading in India:
- **Research:** Learn about different algo trading strategies and understand the risks involved.
- **Choose a Broker:** Select a broker that offers algo trading platforms and caters to your needs. Some popular options include Zerodha Streak, Upstox Pro, and Motilal Oswal ACE FundTech.
- **Practice with Demo Accounts:** Before risking real money, test your algos using a demo account offered by many brokers.

Popular Algo Trading Software in India:
- **Zerodha Streak**: Ideal for back-testing strategies.
- **AlgoTest**: Reliable app for trading.
- **RoboTrade:** Combines automated and manual trading.

- **TradeTron**: Cost-effective algorithmic trading app.
- **Omnesys Nest**: Automated software for Indian markets.
- **MetaTrader 5**: Professional traders' choice.
- **AlgoNomics**: Utilizes multiple trading strategies.
- **EToro Copy** Trading: Allows copying successful traders.
- **AlgoBulls**: Deploys strategies across various assets.

Remember, algo trading can be a complex process. It's crucial to do your research, understand the risks, and start cautiously before venturing into this area of the Indian stock market.

Some Key Risks
1. **Technical Risks:**
    o **Bugs and Glitches**: Errors in algorithm code can lead to unintended trades or financial losses.
    o **Connectivity Issues**: Network failures or server downtime can disrupt execution.
    o **Slippage**: Algorithms may not execute at the desired price due to market volatility.

2. **Market Risks:**

- o **Market Volatility**: Rapid price fluctuations can trigger unexpected trades.
- o **Liquidity Risk**: Illiquid stocks may be hard to exit quickly.
- o **Flash Crashes**: Sudden market drops can impact algorithmic strategies.

3. **Model Risks:**
   - o **Overfitting**: Models may perform well in historical data but fail in real markets.
   - o **Underfitting**: Overly simplistic models may miss profitable opportunities.
   - o **Changing Market Conditions**: Models may not adapt to evolving market dynamics.

4. **Operational Risks:**
   - o **Data Quality**: Garbage in, garbage out—reliable data is crucial.
   - o **Execution Delays**: Latency can affect strategy effectiveness.
   - o **Risk Controls**: Inadequate risk management can lead to large losses.

5. **Behavioral Risks:**

- o **Emotional Bias**: Traders may override algorithms based on fear or greed.
- o **Herding Behavior**: Following popular strategies can lead to crowded trades.
- o **Black Swan Events**: Rare, extreme events can disrupt algorithms.

Remember, thorough testing, risk management protocols, and continuous monitoring are essential for successful algo trading.

Various Charges

1. **Brokerage Fees**:
   - o Brokers charge a fee for executing trades on your behalf. This fee varies based on the brokerage firm and the volume of trades.
   - o Some brokers offer discounted rates for high-frequency traders or those using their proprietary algorithmic trading platforms.

2. **Exchange Transaction Charges**:
   - o Exchanges levy transaction charges for every executed order. These charges depend on the segment (equity, derivatives, commodities) and the order type (intraday, delivery, futures, options).

- o The charges are typically a percentage of the traded value.

3. **Market Data Fees**:
   - o Access to real-time market data (such as stock prices, order book, and historical data) often incurs fees.
   - o Traders using algorithmic strategies require accurate and timely data, which may come at a cost.

4. **Infrastructure Costs**:
   - o Reliable internet connectivity, powerful hardware, and backup systems are essential for algo trading.
   - o These infrastructure costs include internet bills, server hosting, and maintenance.

5. **Software Subscription Fees**:
   - o If you use third-party algorithmic trading software or platforms, there might be subscription fees.
   - o Some brokers provide their own algo trading tools with associated costs.

6. **Back-testing Costs**:

- o Back-testing involves simulating your algorithm on historical data to evaluate its performance.
- o While back-testing tools are available, they may have associated charges.

7. **Risk Management Tools**:
    - o Implementing risk controls (stop-loss, position sizing, etc.) requires additional software or services.
    - o These tools help manage risk but may come with fees.

8. **Taxes and Stamp Duty**:
    - o Algo trades are subject to taxes (such as Securities Transaction Tax) and stamp duty.
    - o These charges vary by state and type of security.

Remember to factor in these costs when planning your algorithmic trading strategy.

Back-testing

Back-testing, in the world of trading, is essentially a method to test the potential effectiveness of a trading strategy before you put your real money on the line. It's like running a simulation to see how your strategy would have performed in the past, given certain historical market conditions.

Here's a breakdown of how it works:
- **Data**: You start with historical price data for the assets you're interested in trading. This data can include things like opening and closing prices, volume, and various technical indicators.
- **Strategy**: You define your trading strategy with specific rules. This could involve using technical indicators, fundamental analysis, or a combination of both, to determine entry and exit points for trades.
- **Simulation**: The back-testing software then simulates how your strategy would have been applied to the historical data. It essentially goes through the data point by point, checking if your entry and exit criteria would have been met, and calculates the potential profits or losses for each trade.

Benefits of Back-testing:
- **Evaluation**: Back-testing allows you to evaluate the performance of your strategy in terms of factors like profitability, win rate, and risk-reward ratio. This helps you identify strengths and weaknesses in your approach.
- **Comparison**: You can compare different trading strategies against each other using the same historical data. This helps you choose the strategy that seems most promising based on past performance.

- **Risk Management**: Back-testing can help you identify potential risks associated with your strategy, such as periods of drawdown or high volatility. This can help you refine your strategy or implement risk management techniques.

Limitations of Back-testing:
- **Past Performance**: It's important to remember that past performance is not always indicative of future results. Markets are constantly changing, and a strategy that worked in the past might not work as well in the future.
- **Overfitting**: Back-testing can lead to overfitting, which is when you optimize your strategy too much to the specific historical data you're using. This can make the strategy appear more effective than it actually is!
- **Real-World Factors**: Back-testing doesn't account for real-world factors that can impact trading, such as slippage (the difference between your intended entry/exit price and the actual price) and emotional biases.

Some popular back-testing tools available in India:

Free Tools:

- **AlgoTest:** AlgoTest offers free back-testing with limitations. It allows back-testing up to 25 strategies per week and specializes in options trading. It has a user-friendly interface and integrates with other platforms like TradingView.

Paid Tools:

- **TradingView:** This popular web-based platform offers a free trial and paid plans with a strategy tester. It uses the Pine Script coding language for back-testing and provides detailed reports on strategy performance.

Advanced Paid Tools:

- **Amibroker:** This comprehensive software is widely used for technical analysis and back-testing. It allows for portfolio-level back-testing and strategy optimization but comes with a steeper learning curve.

- **NinjaTrader 8:** This software caters to advanced traders and allows back-testing and optimization of automated trading strategies.

Broker-specific Platforms:

- **Zerodha Streak:** This cloud-based platform offered by the discount broker Zerodha allows backtesting, strategy development, and live alerts. It has a drag-and-drop interface for creating strategies.

- **Sensibull:** This platform focuses on options trading and provides features for creating and back-testing options strategies.

Choosing the Right Tool:

The best back-testing tool for you depends on your experience level, trading style, and budget. Here are some factors to consider:

- **Experience:** If you're a beginner, consider starting with a free tool like AlgoTest or TradingView's free trial.
- **Trading Style:** Options traders might find AlgoTest or Sensibull valuable, while technical traders might prefer Amibroker or NinjaTrader.
- **Budget:** Free tools are a great starting point, but paid tools often offer more features and flexibility.

Remember, back-testing is just one piece of the puzzle. Always conduct thorough research and understand the limitations of back-testing before deploying your strategies with real money. Overall, back-testing is a valuable tool for traders, but it should be used with caution and in conjunction with other forms of analysis. It's a great way to refine your strategies and gain confidence, but it's not a guarantee of future success.

Cryptocurrencies in India: Risks, Regulations, and Taxes: *Understanding Cryptocurrencies*

Cryptocurrencies are digital or virtual currencies that operate on blockchain technology. They function as a medium of exchange, with transactions recorded on a decentralized ledger.

Popular cryptocurrencies include:
- Bitcoin (BTC)
- Ethereum (ETH)
- Ripple (XRP)
- Litecoin (LTC)

Risks Associated with Cryptocurrencies in India

1. **High Volatility:** Crypto prices can fluctuate dramatically. For example, Bitcoin's price dropped from ₹51,00,000 to ₹26,00,000 between April and July 2021.

2. **Lack of Intrinsic Value:** Cryptocurrencies aren't backed by physical assets or government guarantees.

3. **Cybersecurity Threats:** Crypto exchanges and wallets can be hacked. In 2018, Coinsecure, an Indian exchange, lost bitcoins worth ₹20 crore in a hack.

4. **Regulatory Uncertainty**: The legal status of cryptocurrencies in India has been subject to frequent changes.

5. **Potential for Fraud:** The anonymity of transactions can facilitate scams and Ponzi schemes.

Regulations in India

The regulatory landscape for cryptocurrencies in India has been evolving:

1. **RBI's Stance:** In 2018, the Reserve Bank of India (RBI) banned banks from dealing with crypto businesses. This ban was overturned by the Supreme Court in March 2020.

2. **Proposed Ban**: In 2021, the government considered a bill to ban all private cryptocurrencies, but it wasn't passed.

3. **Current Status:** As of 2024, cryptocurrencies are not illegal, but they're not recognized as legal tender either.

4. **KYC and AML**: Crypto exchanges in India are required to follow Know Your Customer (KYC) and Anti-Money Laundering (AML) guidelines.

5. SEBI Oversight: There are discussions about bringing crypto assets under the purview of the Securities and Exchange Board of India (SEBI).

Future Outlook
The Indian government is working on a regulatory framework for cryptocurrencies. This may include:
- Classification of cryptocurrencies (as commodities, securities, or a new asset class)
- Licensing requirements for crypto exchanges
- Guidelines for institutional investment in crypto assets

Investors and users of cryptocurrencies in India should stay updated with the latest regulations and consult with financial and legal experts for personalized advice.

Tax Implications

Taxation based on Asset Class:
- **Equity (Stocks):** Profits from algo trading in equity are generally considered **capital gains**. These are taxed based on how long you hold the stock (holding period):
    - **Short-term capital gains (STCG):** If you hold the stock for less than one year, your profits are taxed at a flat rate of 20%.
    - **Long-term capital gains (LTCG):** If you hold the stock for more than one

year, LTCGs exceeding ₹1.25 lakh are taxed at 12.5% without any indexation benefit (a mechanism to adjust for inflation).

- **Derivatives (Futures & Options):** Profits from algo trading in derivatives are generally considered **business income**. This means they are added to your total income and taxed according to your income tax slab rate, which can range from 5% to 30%.

Tax Implications for Cryptocurrencies in India

In the 2022 Union Budget, the Indian government introduced a specific tax regime for cryptocurrencies, treating them similarly to speculative income.

- **30% Tax on Income from Cryptocurrencies**: Profits from the sale of cryptocurrencies are taxed at a flat rate of 30%, regardless of the investor's income tax slab. This is one of the highest tax rates and applies to each transaction, not just overall profits.
- **1% TDS on Transactions Above ₹10,000**: A 1% tax deducted at source (TDS) is imposed on transactions above ₹10,000, applicable from July 2022. This applies to every trade, which can affect liquidity and discourage frequent trading.
- **No Offset for Losses**: Losses from cryptocurrency transactions cannot be

offset against other income. For example, if you incur a loss on cryptocurrency trading, you cannot use it to reduce taxable income from other sources, such as stocks or mutual funds.

- **No Deductions**: Unlike other investments, there are no deductions for expenses incurred, except for the cost of acquisition. This can reduce net gains and increase tax liability for active traders.

Additional Factors Affecting Tax Treatment:

- **Trading Frequency:** High-frequency trading activity (especially if your turnover exceeds ₹2 crore in a financial year) might attract scrutiny from tax authorities. They may reclassify your income as business income even for equity trades, potentially leading to higher taxes.
- **Profitability:** If your profits from algo trading in equity are below 6% of your total trading turnover, it's less likely to be classified as business income.

Important Points to Remember:

- **Record Keeping:** Maintain detailed records of your trades, including dates, purchase/sale prices, brokerage fees, and other relevant information. This is crucial for accurate tax filing and claiming deductions for legitimate business expenses.

- **Tax Audit:** If your total income (including algo trading profits) exceeds ₹2.5 lakhs (basic exemption limit) and you have incurred losses or your profits are less than 6% of your turnover, you might be liable for a tax audit.
- **Consult a Tax Advisor:** Algo trading can involve complex tax scenarios. Consider consulting a qualified tax advisor familiar with algo trading regulations in India for personalized guidance based on your specific situation.

By understanding these factors and consulting a professional if needed, you can ensure you're compliant with tax regulations and optimize your tax liability from algo trading in India.

Risk Management Techniques
Here's a breakdown of some key methods:

Planning and Discipline:
- **Define Risk Tolerance:** Before diving in, understand your risk tolerance. How much capital are you comfortable losing on a single trade? The 1% rule suggests risking no more than 1% of your account value per trade.
- **Trading Plan:** Develop a clear trading plan outlining your entry and exit points based on technical analysis, fundamental analysis, or a

combination of both. Stick to the plan and avoid emotional decisions.

Position Sizing and Order Types:
- **Position Sizing:** Control your risk by calculating an appropriate position size for each trade. This could be a fixed percentage of your capital or based on stop-loss levels.
- **Stop-Loss Orders:** Utilize stop-loss orders to automatically exit a losing position at a predetermined price, limiting potential losses.
- **Take-Profit Orders:** Consider take-profit orders to lock in gains when the price reaches your target level.

Portfolio Management:
- **Diversification:** Spread your investments across various asset classes and sectors to mitigate risk. Don't put all your eggs in one basket!
- **Hedging:** For advanced traders, hedging strategies using derivatives like options can help offset potential losses in underlying assets.

Risk Awareness and Monitoring:
- **Market Volatility:** Stay informed about market conditions and economic factors that can impact your trades. Be prepared to

adjust your strategies during periods of high volatility.

- **Money Management:** Maintain a healthy emergency fund outside of your trading capital. Don't invest money you can't afford to lose.
- **Regular Reviews:** Regularly review your portfolio performance and adjust your strategy as needed. Learn from your mistakes and adapt to changing market conditions.

Additional Considerations for India:

- **SEBI Regulations:** Be aware of regulations set by the Securities and Exchange Board of India (SEBI) regarding leverage limits and margin requirements.
- **Brokerage Fees:** Factor in brokerage fees and other trading costs when calculating your potential returns and risk management strategies.

By implementing these risk management techniques, Indian traders can approach the market with a more informed and disciplined strategy, increasing their chances of long-term success. Remember, risk management is an ongoing process, not a one-time fix. Regularly evaluate your approach and adapt as needed to navigate the ever-changing market landscape.

The Dark Side of Algorithmic Trading in India: A Trader Reveals the Risks

My F&O Rollercoaster: A Cautionary Tale

Remember that surge of new traders in F&O everyone was talking about? Yeah, me too. I jumped in 3 years ago, lured by the dream of quick cash. It seemed like everyone was getting rich fast, and who wouldn't want a piece of that pie?

Fortunately, I escaped unscathed—no losses, no gains. The allure of quick profits vanished, replaced by a casino-like atmosphere. Constant screen-watching consumed me, yet the overall returns were meager compared to the effort and capital invested.

Here's the thing they *don't* tell you: most people lose. Big time. Studies show only 1 in 10 traders actually make money, with the average loser down over ₹1.25 lakh! Crazy, right?

So, what's the catch? F&O promises fast riches and lets you control a lot with a little money (leverage). It's exciting, almost addictive. The wins feel amazing, but the losses can be devastating.

Here's the reality I faced:

- **Lack of knowledge:** I didn't fully understand the risks, and there were plenty.
- **Leverage trap:** It can amplify losses just as fast as gains.
- **Mental drain:** The stress and anxiety were constant.
- **Uphill battle:** The odds of long-term success are stacked against you.

I was glued to the screen, constantly chasing the next win. But in the end, for all the effort and risk, the returns were barely there. It felt like a high-stakes game with terrible odds.

Learning about F&O with small amounts is okay, but it's easy to get sucked in. If you see warning signs of addiction, get out. The statistics don't lie. F&O just isn't worth the risk for most people.

So, have you tried F&O trading? Think carefully before you do. There are better ways to grow your wealth.

FOOD FOR THOUGHT

"True financial freedom in the stock market isn't about chasing quick gains, but about exercising patience and letting your investments grow steadily over time."

Chapter 12 - AI Tools

AI tools are basically computer programs that are super good at learning and doing specific tasks, kind of like how we humans learn from experience.

Here's a breakdown:
Simple Explanation:
- Imagine a super smart calculator that can get better at things the more it's used.
- That's kind of like an AI tool. It uses data and instructions to learn and improve at a specific task.

Detailed Explanation:
- AI stands for Artificial Intelligence. It's a field of computer science focused on making machines mimic human intelligence.
- AI tools are software applications that use this technology.
- These tools can learn from data, identify patterns, and make decisions based on what they've learned.

There are many different types of AI tools, each with its own specialty. Here are some examples:
- **Image recognition tools:** These can identify objects in pictures and videos, like spotting a cat in a photo.

- **Chatbots:** These are computer programs that can have conversations with people, like answering questions on a website.
- **Recommendation systems:** These suggest things you might like based on your past behavior, like movie recommendations on streaming services.

AI tools are becoming increasingly common and are used in many different fields, such as:

- **Healthcare:** AI can analyze medical images to help doctors diagnose diseases.
- **Finance:** AI can be used to detect fraud and make investment decisions.
- **Transportation:** Self-driving cars use AI to navigate the roads.

Things to keep in mind:

- AI tools are still under development, and they can sometimes make mistakes.
- It's important to use them responsibly and ethically.

Popular AI tools

AI tools have become increasingly popular and diverse, transforming various industries. Here are some notable ones:

1. **ChatGPT:** This ubiquitous AI chatbot, based on a large language model (LLM), provides detailed responses in natural, human-like language. It's used by over two million

developers and at least 92% of Fortune 500 companies.

2. **Claude AI**: Developed by Anthropic, Claude excels in text-based tasks, coding, infographics, chart creation, and more. Its latest version, Claude 3.5 Sonnet, has garnered attention on Twitter.

3. **Google Gemini**: A collaborative chatbot that sources information from the web, Gemini was trained on Google's own LLMs. It boasts a massive training dataset and millions of users per month.

4. **Synthesia**: This browser-based AI software creates engaging videos from plain text, featuring customizable avatars and narration in multiple languages.

5. **Anyword**: Ideal for writing support, Anyword uses AI to enhance content creation and copywriting.

6. **Jasper**: An AI-powered marketing content tool that streamlines content generation.

7. **Runway**: Perfect for creative videos, Runway offers freeform video creation using AI.

8. **Wondershare Filmora**: Enhance videos with AI-generated effects and polish.

9. **Adobe Photoshop**: Leverage AI for image enhancement and manipulation.

Remember, the right tool depends on your specific needs, so explore and find what suits you best!

AI use cases in Healthcare Industry
Artificial intelligence (AI) is revolutionizing healthcare across various domains. Here are some impactful use cases:

1. **Medical Diagnosis and Treatment**:
- AI aids in diagnosing diseases and recommending treatment plans based on patient data and scientific literature.
- It augments clinician knowledge by analyzing patient information.

2. **Patient Data Processing**:
- AI efficiently processes large volumes of patient data, improving data management and decision-making.

3. **Medical Imaging Analysis**:
- AI algorithms enhance medical imaging interpretation, assisting radiologists in detecting anomalies and diagnosing conditions.

4. **Electronic Health Records (EHRs)**:
- AI optimizes EHRs by automating data entry, improving accuracy, and facilitating information retrieval.

5. **Remote Patient Assistance**:
- AI-powered telemedicine tools enable remote consultations, monitoring, and personalized care.

6. **Virtual Assistants and Chatbots**:
- AI-driven chatbots provide instant responses, appointment scheduling, and health-related information.

7. **Drug Discovery & Vaccine Research**:
- AI accelerates drug discovery by analyzing molecular data, predicting drug interactions, and identifying potential candidates.

Remember, these applications demonstrate how AI is transforming healthcare delivery, improving patient outcomes, and streamlining processes!

Business use cases

Businesses are increasingly leveraging artificial intelligence (AI) tools to enhance their operations and improve efficiency. Here are some key applications:

1. **Customer Service:** AI chatbots like ChatGPT are widely used for automating responses and improving service quality.
2. **Cybersecurity and Fraud Management:** AI helps detect and respond to real-time threats, safeguarding businesses from security breaches.

3. **Customer Relationship Management (CRM)**: AI assists in managing customer interactions and analyzing data.
4. **Digital Personal Assistants**: These AI tools aid in tasks such as scheduling, reminders, and information retrieval.
5. **Inventory Management:** AI optimizes inventory levels, reducing costs and ensuring efficient supply chains.
6. **Content Production:** AI generates written content, including website articles, marketing materials, and social media posts.
7. **Product Recommendations**: AI algorithms analyze user behavior to provide personalized product suggestions.
8. **Accounting**: AI streamlines financial processes, automating tasks like invoice processing and expense tracking.
9. **Supply Chain Operations:** AI enhances logistics, demand forecasting, and inventory management.
10. **Recruitment and Talent Sourcing:** AI tools assist in identifying suitable candidates and streamlining hiring processes.

Remember, the right AI tool depends on the specific needs of each business.

Share Market Trading and Investments use cases

AI is making waves in the world of finance, particularly in share market trading and investments. Here's how AI is being used in this domain:

- **High-Frequency Trading (HFT):** AI algorithms excel at analyzing massive amounts of data at lightning speed. This allows them to exploit short-term market movements for profitable trades, something traditional methods struggle with.
- **Pattern Recognition:** AI can sift through years of historical data to identify trading patterns and trends. These patterns can then be used to predict future price movements and inform investment decisions.
- **Sentiment Analysis:** AI can analyze news articles, social media posts, and other forms of communication to gauge investor sentiment towards specific companies or sectors. This sentiment analysis can help investors make informed decisions about buying or selling stocks.
- **Algorithmic Trading:** AI can be used to develop complex trading algorithms that automatically execute trades based on predefined criteria. This removes emotions from the decision-making process and ensures consistent execution of trading strategies.

- **Portfolio Optimization:** AI can analyze an investor's risk tolerance and financial goals to recommend optimal portfolio allocations. This helps investors build diversified portfolios that align with their risk profile.
- **Fraud Detection:** AI can be used to identify unusual trading patterns that might indicate fraudulent activity. This helps protect investors and maintain the integrity of the market.

Here are some advantages of using AI in share market trading and investments:

- **Reduced Costs:** AI can automate tasks and eliminate the need for human intervention, potentially reducing investment management fees.
- **Increased Efficiency:** AI can analyze vast amounts of data and identify patterns much faster than humans, leading to more efficient investment decisions.
- **Reduced Emotions:** AI removes emotions from the trading process, which can lead to more objective and rational investment decisions.

It's important to remember that AI is still under development and has limitations. Here are some things to keep in mind:

- **AI is not perfect:** AI algorithms can make mistakes, especially with unforeseen market conditions.
- **Over-reliance on AI:** Investors should not solely rely on AI for making investment decisions. Human expertise and judgment are still crucial.
- **Data Bias:** AI algorithms are only as good as the data they are trained on. Biases in the data can lead to biased investment recommendations.

Overall, AI presents exciting opportunities for the share market and investment world. However, it's important to use this technology responsibly and be aware of its limitations.

FOOD FOR THOUGHT

" Embracing AI tools isn't just about staying ahead—it's about amplifying your financial freedom with precision and speed that was once the realm of science fiction. "

Chapter 13 - Multiple Sources of Income

Multiple sources of income refer to having income coming in from more than one place. This can include a mix of earned (through active work) and passive income (earned with less ongoing effort).

Why Multiple Income Streams?
- **Financial Security:** Imagine if your main source of income dries up due to job loss, economic downturn, or illness. Multiple income streams create a safety net, ensuring some income keeps flowing even if one source falters.
- **Increased Earning Potential:** With multiple income sources, you're not limited to the earning potential of a single job. You can leverage your skills and interests to bring in extra income.
- **Reach Financial Goals Faster:** Multiple income streams can help you achieve financial goals like saving for a house, retirement, or that dream vacation quicker.
- **Flexibility and Freedom:** Having additional income streams can give you more control over your time. You might be able to work less or pursue more flexible work arrangements.

Examples of Income Streams

- ○ **Dividend Stocks**: Invest in companies that distribute profits to shareholders as dividends.
- ○ **High-Yield Savings Accounts (HYSA)**: Earn interest on your savings with minimal risk.
- ○ **Real Estate Investing**: Buy properties for rental income or capital appreciation.
- ○ **Side Gigs**: Freelancing, tutoring, or consulting can provide extra income.
- ○ **P2P Lending**: Lend money to individuals or businesses for interest.
- ○ **Broker Partner**: Collaboration can open access to a wider range of financial products and lenders for your clients.
- ○ **Insurance Advisor**: Earn money through commissions on policy sales and can charge fees for consultative services.
- ○ **Affiliate marketing**: Performance-based marketing strategy where you (the affiliate) can earn a commission by promoting another company's product or service.
- ○ **Mystery Shopping**: Get paid to evaluate customer experiences.

- **Renting Out Assets**: Rent out a spare room, car, or equipment.

Earned Income vs Passive Income

Here are some examples of different income streams:

- **Earned Income:** Salary from a job, freelancing fees, commissions from sales.
- **Passive Income:** Rental income from property, royalties from creative work, investment returns.

Choosing Your Streams:

- Consider your risk tolerance, available time, and desired returns.
- Passive income requires less effort but may yield lower returns.
- Active income involves more work but can be lucrative.

Choosing the Right Mix:

The ideal mix of income streams depends on your individual goals, risk tolerance, and resources. Some options require upfront investment (like real estate), while others require ongoing effort (like freelancing).

Remember: Building additional income streams often takes time and effort. Do your research and choose options that align with your skills and interests.

FOOD FOR THOUGHT

"In today's unpredictable economy, relying on a single income source is like walking a tightrope without a safety net—diversify to secure your financial future."

Chapter 14 - Real estate

Homeownership in India carries a lot of weight beyond just bricks and mortar. Here's a breakdown of the concept and its emotional ties:

What is Homeownership?
In India, homeownership typically refers to owning a house or apartment. This can be achieved through full payment or a mortgage, which is a loan to pay for the property over time.

Emotional Impact:
- **Security and Stability:** Owning a home provides a sense of security and stability, knowing you have a permanent place to live that isn't subject to rent hikes or the whims of a landlord. This can significantly reduce stress and anxiety.

- **Sense of Belonging:** A home is more than just shelter; it's a place to personalize and express yourself. Decorating and making it your own strengthens the emotional bond with the space, fostering a true sense of belonging.

- **Financial Security:** Homeownership is seen as a path to building wealth. As you pay off the mortgage, you gain equity in the property, which can be a valuable asset. This financial security contributes to overall well-being.

- **Pride and Achievement:** Owning a home is a significant milestone in India, signifying success, and social status. It's a source of pride for individuals and families, reflecting hard work and accomplishment.

Challenges to Consider:
The journey to homeownership can be stressful, especially in India's competitive real estate market. High property prices and lengthy loan processes can cause anxiety. Additionally, the financial responsibility of maintaining a home can be a burden for some.

Overall, homeownership in India is deeply tied to emotions. It represents security, stability, achievement, and a sense of belonging. However, the road to getting there can be challenging.

Buying land as an investment
While land can be a good long-term investment, there are definitely some drawbacks to consider before you dive in:

Liquidity Concerns: Land is a much less liquid asset compared to stocks or bonds. It can take months or even years to find a buyer, especially for undeveloped land or in a slow market. This can be a problem if you need to access your money quickly.

Limited Immediate Returns: Unlike rental properties, vacant land doesn't generate any income. You'll only see a return on your investment when you eventually sell it, which could be a long time down the road.

Development Challenges: Even if you plan to develop the land, there can be hurdles. Zoning restrictions, obtaining permits, and infrastructure needs can all add time and expense to your project.

Carrying Costs: Property taxes still apply to vacant land. These ongoing costs eat into your potential profits.

Risk of Undeveloped Potential: Land value hinges on future development in the area. If the surrounding area doesn't develop as expected, your land may not appreciate in value as much as you'd hoped.

Legal and Ownership Issues: It's crucial to do thorough due diligence before buying land. This includes verifying ownership titles, checking for potential encroachments, and ensuring the land is zoned for your intended use.

Environmental Concerns: Be aware of any potential environmental hazards on the property, such as soil contamination or flooding risks. These can significantly impact the value and future use of the land.

Investing in Apartment for additional income

Here are some drawbacks to consider before buying a second apartment flat for investment in India:

- **High upfront cost:** A second property requires a significant initial investment, including the down payment, registration fees, and potentially stamp duty. This can limit your ability to invest in other areas.
- **Illiquidity:** Real estate is a relatively illiquid asset. Selling an apartment can take time, especially in a slow market. This can be inconvenient if you need to access the capital quickly.
- **Management responsibility:** As a landlord, you'll be responsible for finding tenants, managing repairs and maintenance, and dealing with potential vacancies. This can be time-consuming and require additional expenses.
- **Rental income uncertainty:** Rental yields (income as a percentage of property value) in India can vary depending on location and property type. There's no guarantee you'll find tenants consistently, and vacancy periods can affect your returns.

- **Market fluctuations:** The real estate market can be cyclical. Property values may not always appreciate as expected, and there's a risk of facing a loss if you need to sell during a downturn.
- **Maintenance costs:** Owning a second property comes with ongoing maintenance expenses, including property taxes, society maintenance charges, and potential repairs. These costs can eat into your rental income.
- **Tax implications:** In India, capital gains tax applies to profits earned from the sale of a property held for more than a year. This can impact your overall return on investment.
- **Diversification:** Concentrating a large portion of your investment portfolio in real estate limits diversification. This can increase your overall risk profile.

Here are some additional factors to consider:
- **Location:** Carefully research the location of the property. Look for areas with strong rental demand and potential for future growth.
- **Property type:** Consider the type of apartment that would be most attractive to tenants in your chosen location.
- **Your financial situation:** Ensure you have a healthy emergency fund and sufficient cash flow to cover the mortgage payments,

maintenance costs, and potential vacancies without straining your finances.

It's important to weigh the potential drawbacks against the benefits of buying a second apartment for investment. Consider consulting a financial advisor to discuss your specific situation and determine if this is the right investment strategy for you.

Real Estate returns

Historical real estate returns in India can vary depending on the specific property, location, and investment type (direct ownership vs REITs). Here's a general breakdown:

- **Direct Ownership:** Long-term studies suggest historical appreciation of around 7-9% annually. Anecdotal evidence can show higher figures, but keep in mind those are specific cases.

- **REITs (since 2014):** These offer a mix of rental income (around 8-10% annually) and capital appreciation (around 5% per year on average).

Remember that real estate investments involve various costs (maintenance, taxes, etc.) and illiquidity. Always conduct thorough research and consider professional advice before making investment decisions.

REITs

Real Estate Investment Trusts (REITs) in India are an innovative investment avenue that bridges the gap between real estate and stock markets. Here's an overview:

1. **Nature and Purpose:**
   - REITs are private trusts registered with SEBI (Securities and Exchange Board of India).
   - They primarily invest in completed, revenue-generating real estate assets within India.
   - Earnings from these assets are distributed to unit-holders.

2. **Structure:**
   - REITs are listed on stock exchanges.
   - Investors can buy units of REITs, which represent ownership in the underlying real estate portfolio.

3. **Benefits:**
   - Diversification: Access to a diversified real estate portfolio.
   - Liquidity: Units can be bought or sold easily on stock exchanges.

     o Income: Regular income through rental yields.

4. **Risks:**
   - o Market Risk: REIT prices can fluctuate due to market conditions.
   - o Property Risk: Performance depends on the quality of underlying assets.

5. **Eligibility:**
   - o Any investor with substantial capital can invest in REITs.

Remember to research specific REITs and consider your investment goals before diving in.

Overall comparison

Feature	Real Estate	REITs	Equity
Investment type	Physical property	Company shares	Company shares
Minimum investment	High	Lower	Variable
Liquidity	Low (illiquid)	High (liquid)	High (liquid)
Returns	Rental income, capital	Dividends, capital appreciation	Capital appreciation, dividends

	appreciation		(optional)
Historical returns	4-7%	8-12%	>12%
Management responsibility	High (landlord duties)	Low (professional management)	Low
Risk	High (vacancy, market fluctuations)	Moderate (market fluctuations, REIT performance)	Moderate (market fluctuations, company performance)

FOOD FOR THOUGHT

"Real estate can be a solid investment, but remember: bricks and mortar don't pay the bills. It's the income they generate that matter."

Chapter 15 - Tax Planning

Direct vs Indirect Taxes

In India, taxes are broadly classified into two categories: **direct taxes** and **indirect taxes**. Here's a concise explanation of each:

Direct Taxes

Direct taxes are levied directly on the income or wealth of individuals or organizations. The taxpayer pays these taxes directly to the government, and the burden of the tax cannot be shifted to someone else. Some common examples include:

- **Income Tax**: Imposed on the income earned by individuals and businesses.
- **Capital Gains Tax**: Levied on the profit from the sale of assets or investments.
- **Securities Transaction Tax (STT)**: Charged on transactions in securities (like stocks).

Pros:

- Helps in reducing income inequality.
- Directly increases government revenue.

Cons:

- Can be complex to administer and collect.
- High potential for tax evasion.

Indirect Taxes

Indirect taxes are levied on goods and services rather than on income or profits. These taxes are collected by an intermediary (like a retailer) from the consumer, who ultimately bears the tax burden. Examples include:

- **Goods and Services Tax (GST)**: A comprehensive tax on the manufacture, sale, and consumption of goods and services.
- **Customs Duty**: Imposed on goods imported into the country.
- **Excise Duty**: Levied on the manufacture of goods within the country.

Pros:

- Easier to collect as they are included in the price of goods and services.
- Broader tax base as they are paid by all consumers.

Cons:

- Can be regressive, affecting lower-income individuals more.
- May lead to higher prices for consumers.

Both types of taxes are essential for the government's revenue and play a crucial role in the country's economic structure.

Tax rates in India
Income Tax Regimes for FY 2024-2025 (AY 2025-2026)

India offers two income tax regimes for individuals:

1. Old Tax Regime

This is the traditional tax regime with various deductions and exemptions.

Tax Slabs:

- Income up to Rs. 2,50,000: Nil
- Income from Rs. 2,50,000 to Rs. 5,00,000: 5%
- Income from Rs. 5,00,000 to Rs. 10,00,000: 20%
- Income from Rs. 10,00,000 to Rs. 12,50,000: 30%
- Income above Rs. 12,50,000: 30% + Surcharge + Cess

Key Features:

- Allows various deductions under Chapter VI-A like Section 80C, 80D, etc.
- Complex calculations due to multiple slabs and deductions.

2. New Tax Regime

Tax Slabs rates for FY 2025-26:

- Income up to Rs. 4,00,000: Nil
- Income from Rs. 4,00,000 to Rs. 8,00,000: 5%
- Income from Rs. 8,00,000 to Rs. 12,00,000: 10%

- Income from Rs. 12,00,000 to Rs. 16,00,000: 15%
- Income from Rs. 16,00,000 to Rs. 20,00,000: 20%
- Income from Rs. 20,00,000 to Rs. 24,00,000: 25%
- Income above Rs. 24,00,000: 30%

Key Features:
- Simpler tax calculations with fewer slabs.
- Limited deductions and exemptions.

Choosing the Right Regime

The best regime for you depends on your income, deductions, and financial situation.

- **Opt for the New Regime** if you have minimal deductions and a straightforward income source.
- **Consider the Old Regime** if you have significant deductions like home loan interest, investments, medical expenses, etc.

Important Note:
- The Finance Act, 2023 has made the new tax regime the default option. If you prefer the old regime, you need to explicitly opt for it.

Additional Considerations:
- **Surcharge and Cess:** Applicable on both regimes based on your total income.

- **Rebate under Section 87A:** Available in both regimes for incomes up to Rs. 5 lakhs.
- **Standard Deduction:** Available in both regimes.

It's recommended to use income tax calculators or consult a tax professional to determine the most beneficial regime for your specific financial situation.

Corporate Tax Rates

1. Domestic Companies:
   - Turnover up to ₹400 crore: 25%
   - Turnover above ₹400 crore: 30%
2. Foreign Companies: 40%

Capital Gains Tax Rates

1. Short-Term Capital Gains (STCG):
   - Equity-oriented funds: 20%
   - Other assets: As per the individual's income tax slab rates

2. Long-Term Capital Gains (LTCG):
   - Equity-oriented funds: 12.5% (for gains exceeding ₹1.25 lakh)
   - Other assets: 12.5% without indexation benefits

Real Estate Investments

There's been a significant change in the tax rates for long-term capital gains (LTCG) on real estate.

Previously, the LTCG on real estate was taxed at 20% with indexation benefits. Indexation helped adjust the purchase price for inflation, reducing the taxable gain.

Now, taxpayers have a choice:
1. **20% LTCG tax with indexation benefit:** This is the old regime.
2. **12.5% LTCG tax without indexation benefit:** This is the new regime.

Which option is better?
The optimal choice depends on various factors, including:
- **When you purchased the property:** If you purchased it long ago, indexation benefits can be substantial, making the 20% option more attractive.
- **Your overall income tax slab:** If you're in a higher tax bracket, the lower 12.5% rate might be beneficial even without indexation.

It's crucial to calculate the tax liability under both options to make an informed decision.

Note: This change is applicable to properties purchased before July 23, 2024.

Other Income
1. **Interest Income:** Taxed as per the individual's income tax slab rates.

2. **Rental Income**: Taxed as per the individual's income tax slab rates.
3. **Dividend Income**: Taxed as per the individual's income tax slab rates.

These rates are subject to applicable surcharges and cess.

National Pension Scheme (NPS): A Retirement Savings Plan

The National Pension System (NPS) is a government-backed retirement savings scheme designed to help individuals build a corpus for their post-retirement life. It's regulated by the Pension Fund Regulatory and Development Authority (PFRDA).

Two Types of Accounts:

- **Tier I Account**: This is a mandatory, non-withdrawable account meant for retirement savings.
- **Tier II Account:** This is a voluntary savings account from which you can withdraw funds anytime, but it does not offer tax benefits.

How Does it Work?

- **Defined Contribution:** Unlike traditional pension schemes, NPS is a defined contribution plan. This means you and/or your employer contribute a specific amount to your pension account.

- **Investment Options:** Your contributions are invested in a diversified portfolio of assets like government securities, corporate bonds, and equities.
- **Professional Management:** Your investments are managed by professional fund managers.
- **Tax Benefits:** You can avail tax benefits under Sections 80C and 80CCD of the Income Tax Act on your contributions.
- **Portability:** Your NPS account can be transferred even if you change jobs or relocate.

Benefits of NPS

- **Tax Benefits**: As mentioned, NPS offers tax benefits under Sections 80C and 80CCD of the Income Tax Act.
- **Market-Linked Returns:** Your investments are market-linked, which means you have the potential to earn higher returns compared to traditional pension schemes.
- **Diversification**: Your investments are spread across different asset classes, reducing risk.
- **Flexibility**: You have the option to choose investment options based on your risk appetite.
- **Portability:** You can carry your NPS account with you even if you change jobs or cities.
- **Low Costs:** NPS has relatively low management fees.

How to Withdraw?

At retirement, you have two options:

- **Annuity:** A portion of your accumulated corpus is used to purchase an annuity, which provides a regular income for life.
- **Lump Sum:** The remaining amount can be withdrawn as a lump sum.

Important Note: At least 40% of your accumulated corpus must be used to purchase an annuity.

Eligibility

Any Indian citizen between the ages of 18 and 70 can open an NPS account.

FOOD FOR THOUGHT

" Don't let taxes eat away at your financial freedom. Plan wisely and reap the rewards. "

Chapter 16 - Cyber Crimes and Scams

Cyber Crimes: A Digital Threat

Cybercrime refers to any criminal activity that involves computers and networks. It can range from simple fraud to complex attacks on government and corporate infrastructure. The digital age has made it easier for criminals to operate globally, making cybercrime a significant challenge.

Main Types of Cybercrimes in India

India, like many other countries, is grappling with a rising tide of cybercrime. Some of the most prevalent types include:

Financial Cybercrimes

- **Phishing:** Deceiving users into revealing personal information through fraudulent emails or websites.
- **Online Banking Fraud:** Unauthorized access to bank accounts for financial gain.
- **Credit Card Fraud:** Misuse of credit card information for unauthorized transactions.
- **Online Auction Fraud:** Scams related to online buying and selling platforms.

Cyber Stalking and Harassment

- **Cyberstalking:** Persistent harassment or threats through digital platforms.
- **Online Harassment:** Abusive or threatening behavior online, including cyberbullying.

Data Theft and Privacy Violations

- **Identity Theft:** Stealing personal information to impersonate someone.
- **Data Breach:** Unauthorized access to sensitive data.
- **Meddling with Computer System:** Unauthorized access or modification of computer systems.

Intellectual Property Theft

- **Software Piracy:** Illegal copying and distribution of software.
- **Copyright Infringement:** Unauthorized use of copyrighted material.

Cyber Terrorism

- **Cyber Attacks:** Targeting critical infrastructure or government systems to disrupt services.
- **Spreading Disinformation:** Disseminating false information to create panic or instability.

Other Cybercrimes

- **Child Pornography:** Distribution and possession of child sexual abuse material.
- **Cyber Extortion:** Demanding money or other valuable assets through threats.
- **Online Gambling:** Illegal online betting activities.

It's important to note that this is not an exhaustive list, and new types of cybercrimes emerge constantly.

Prevention and Protection

To protect yourself from cybercrime, it's crucial to:

- Be cautious about clicking on unknown links or downloading attachments.
- Use strong, unique passwords for online accounts.
- Keep your software and operating system updated.
- Be mindful of sharing personal information online.
- Regularly back up your data.

For businesses, implementing robust cybersecurity measures, employee training, and incident response plans are essential.

Scams: The Art of Deception

A **scam** is a fraudulent scheme designed to deceive people for financial gain or other benefits.

Scammers often exploit trust, fear, or greed to manipulate their victims. With the rise of technology, scams have become increasingly sophisticated and widespread.

Main Types of Scams in India

India has witnessed a surge in various scams, targeting individuals and businesses alike. Here are some common types:

Financial Scams

- **Phishing:** Deceiving individuals into revealing personal information through fraudulent emails, messages, or websites.
- **Investment Scams:** Promising unrealistically high returns on investments, often involving Ponzi schemes or fake companies.
- **Loan Scams:** Offering easy loans with hidden charges or fraudulent terms.
- **Insurance Fraud:** False claims or misrepresentation of facts to obtain insurance benefits.

Online Scams

- **E-commerce Fraud:** Fake online stores or fraudulent transactions.
- **Social Media Scams:** Impersonating individuals or businesses to gain personal information or money.
- **Online Dating Scams:** Creating fake profiles to build trust and then defraud victims.

Other Scams

- **Job Scams:** Promising lucrative jobs in exchange for upfront fees.
- **Lottery Scams:** Claiming that the victim has won a lottery and demanding upfront fees to claim the prize.
- **Charity Scams:** Soliciting donations for fake charities.

It's important to note that this is not an exhaustive list, and new scam variations emerge frequently.

Protection Against Scams

To safeguard yourself from scams, follow these tips:

- Be wary of unsolicited offers promising quick riches or easy loans.
- Verify the authenticity of any communication before sharing personal or financial information.
- Use strong, unique passwords for online accounts.
- Be cautious about clicking on links or downloading attachments from unknown sources.
- Educate yourself about common scams and how to identify them.

FOOD FOR THOUGHT

" Don't let cyber frauds steal your financial dreams—stay informed and secure. "

Charity: A Cornerstone of Humanity

Charity, the selfless act of giving to those in need, is a cornerstone of a compassionate society. It's more than just a monetary contribution; it's a profound expression of empathy and human connection.

By extending a helping hand, individuals contribute to a ripple effect of positive change. Charity strengthens communities, bridges divides, and addresses pressing social issues. It's a powerful tool for fostering a more just and equitable world.

The rewards of charitable acts are manifold. Beyond the gratification of making a difference, it enriches our lives with purpose and meaning. Studies have shown that giving back boosts happiness, reduces stress, and strengthens social bonds.

Whether it's volunteering time, donating resources, or offering support, every act of charity counts. Let's embrace the spirit of giving and create a world where compassion thrives.

Remember, charity isn't about the size of the donation, but the intent behind it. Every contribution, no matter how small, can make a significant impact.

About Author

Parthiban Viswanathan is an entrepreneur and financial freedom coach based in Chennai, Tamil Nadu, with over five years of experience helping professionals achieve financial freedom. In 2019, he founded the Financial Freedom Club to support busy individuals in attaining financial independence through simple and time-efficient investment strategies. His approach is centered on developing personalized financial plans that align with each person's unique goals, making wealth management more accessible.

His mission is to empower one lakh families to build lasting wealth and reach early retirement. He is certified in NISM VA - Mutual Funds Distribution and an IRDA Certified Insurance Advisor.

Fluent in Tamil and English, he is deeply committed to fostering financial literacy and contributing to the greater good. His goal is to help individuals and communities achieve lasting financial security. Let's connect and work together toward a financially secure future.

Author can be reached out through mail -
parthiban_v89@hotmail.com
Personal website - https://parthibanviswanathan.com/

Registration Details
AMFI Certified Mutual Funds Distributor
ARN: 256950

IRDA Certified Life Insurance Advisor and Health Planner
ILN: 20684066

Certified as a Retirement Specialist by CIEL
Awarded an Entrepreneurship Certificate by the Government of India

www.ingramcontent.com/pod-product-compliance
Lightning Source LLC
Chambersburg PA
CBHW051224130726

47988CB00001B/215